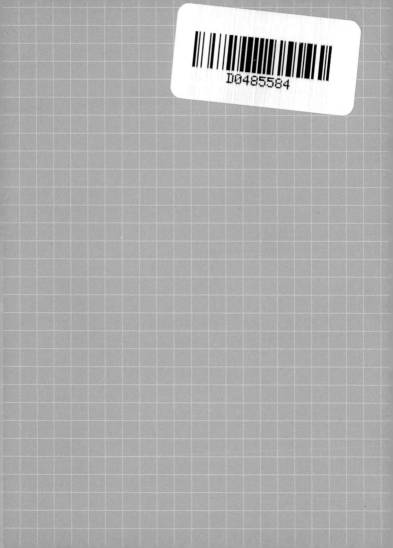

DO ONE THING EVERY DAY THAT MAKES YOU SMARTER

A Journal for Lifelong Learners

I am still learning.

Michelangelo

This was a favorite saying of one of the greatest artists of all time. And modern science has proved him right. Neuroplasticity—the ability of the brain to change throughout adulthood—was one of the great discoveries of the late 20th century. "We come into the world programmed with the capacity to change what is given to us by nature, so that we can go beyond it," according to cognitive neuroscientist Maryanne Wolf. "Groups of neurons," she writes, "create new connections and pathways among themselves every time we acquire a new skill."

The psychologist Howard Gardner introduced the Theory of Multiple Intelligences in the 1980s. He identified eight different ways in which we can excel at processing information—at being smart—from the linguistic to the musical, only three of which are measured by standard IQ tests.

What better way is there to take advantage of both Wolf's and Gardner's insights than to accept the challenge of this book to *do one thing every day that makes you smarter*? Prompts activate all of your intelligences in response to the words of brilliant poets, artists, entertainers, writers, actors, scientists, politicians, and philosophers. Skim through the book's pages each day to find a way to expand your mind that interests you.

Compare yourself to underestimated geniuses like Thomas Edison, who was once told by a teacher that he was "too stupid to learn anything." Discover secrets to getting smarter from "MacArthur geniuses," winners of an award given by the MacArthur Foundation for "extraordinary originality and dedication . . . and a marked capacity for self-direction." Flex your brain with word, number, and optical puzzles, and pledge to add to your knowledge from lists of key information in a range of fields from classic films to contemporary technology skills. Read about the "Aha!" moments of Stephen Hawking, Oprah Winfrey, and others, and record Aha! moments of your own. Find tips for how to work, study, eat, and even sound smarter. Gain insight into your own mind by reflecting on what you know and don't know.

This book is not just a collection of the wise words of others, however. It is a place where you can put your own ideas into words. "The finest thought runs the risk of being irrevocably forgotten," wrote the philosopher Arthur Schopenhauer, "if we do not write it down."

Begin with the report card on this page: Grade how smart you feel today. Then grade yourself again at the end of the last page of the book—after a year of *doing one thing every day that makes you smarter.*

DATE: __ / __ / __

How smart do you feel today?

_____

Give yourself a grade: ☐ A

☐ B

☐ C

☐ D

☐ F

☐ Incomplete

You are braver than you believe, stronger than you seem, and smarter than you think.

A. A. Milne

I might be smarter than I thought because today I:

_____

_____

_____

_____

_____

Being smart is cooler than anything in the world.

Michelle Obama

How my smarts made me feel cool today:

_____

_____

_____

_____

_____

DID YOU SHOW

MORE PROMISE THAN

ALBERT EINSTEIN,

the Nobel-Prize-winning physicist?

He didn't talk until he was four and didn't read until he was seven. His teachers thought he was slow.

When did you learn to talk? _____

To read? _____

How would you rank yourself from 1 to 10 (low to high) as a talker now?

_____

As a reader? _____

DATE: __ / __ / __

Imagination is more important than knowledge.

Albert Einstein

How I used my imagination to solve a problem today:

_____

_____

_____

_____

_____

_____

To attain
knowledge,
add things
every day.
To attain wisdom,
subtract things
every day.

Lao-tzu

DATE: __ / __ / __

WHAT I ADDED TO BECOME MORE KNOWLEDGEABLE TODAY:

_____

_____

_____

_____

_____

_____

DATE: __ / __ / __

WHAT I SUBTRACTED TO BECOME WISER TODAY:

_____

_____

_____

_____

_____

The true University of these days is a Collection of Books.

Thomas Carlyle

My University library:

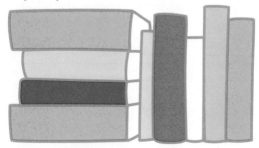

Already Read   To Be Read

A whale-ship was my Yale College and my Harvard.

Herman Melville

What I learned on the sea of life today:

_____

_____

_____

_____

_____

_____

WORK SMART:

Easy-to-Remember Strategies

K. Keep

I. It

S. Simple

S. Stupid

Today I kept this simple:

Only great minds can afford a simple style.

Stendhal, attributed

I did this in a simple style today:

_____

_____

_____

_____

_____

_____

Find the two men in the visual illusion below.
How would you describe them?

(See *Solutions to Puzzles* at the back of the book.)

TAKE ADVANTAGE OF THE AMBIGUITY IN THE WORLD. LOOK AT SOMETHING AND THINK WHAT ELSE IT MIGHT BE.

Roger von Oech

Turn this tape dispenser into a snail or something else:

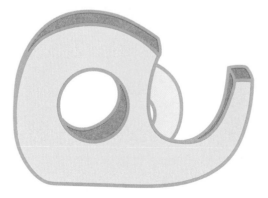

DATE: __ / __ / __

MY 1 PERCENT INSPIRATION TODAY:

_____

_____

_____

_____

_____

_____

DATE: __ / __ / __

MY 99 PERCENT PERSPIRATION TODAY:

_____

_____

_____

_____

_____

_____

Genius is
1 percent
inspiration
and
99 percent
perspiration.

Thomas Alva Edison

Let us not underrate the value of a fact; it will one day flower in a truth.

Henry David Thoreau

Today _____

(a fact)

flowered in _____.

(a truth)

The facts are to blame, my friend. We are all imprisoned by facts.

Luigi Pirandello

I used to be imprisoned by this fact:

_____

_____

Today I escaped from it by:

_____

_____

Susan A Murphy, MacArthur Fellow

The one thing I do every day that makes me smarter is exercise! Exercise helps me to think more critically and with greater focus. Find your exercise.

My exercise:
- ☐ tennis
- ☐ soccer
- ☐ karate
- ☐ dance
- ☐ ice hockey (Susan A. Murphy)
- ☐ other: _____

GIVE ABOUT TWO [HOURS],
EVERY DAY, TO EXERCISE. . . .
A STRONG BODY MAKES
THE MIND STRONG.

Thomas Jefferson

I gave _____ hours to exercise today.

DATE: __/__/__

10 FILMS
SMART PEOPLE KNOW

☐ *2001: A Space Odyssey*

☐ *Apocalypse Now*

☐ *Casablanca*

☐ *Citizen Kane*

☐ *City Lights*

☐ *The Godfather*

☐ *Gone with the Wind*

☐ *Notorious*

☐ *Singin' in the Rain*

☐ *Star Wars: Episode 1*

The film I plan to see next:

Every great film should seem new every time you see it.

Roger Ebert

Choose a film from the list to rewatch:

_____

Something new about a character that I noticed this time:

_____

_____

_____

_____

_____

A GENIUS
IS A MAN
WHO HAS
TWO GREAT
IDEAS.

Jacob Bronowski

DATE: __ / __ / __

MY GENIUS IDEA #1:

_____

_____

_____

_____

_____

_____

DATE: __ / __ / __

MY GENIUS IDEA #2:

_____

_____

_____

_____

_____

_____

THAT IS WHAT LEARNING IS.
YOU SUDDENLY UNDERSTAND
SOMETHING YOU'VE UNDERSTOOD
ALL YOUR LIFE, BUT IN A NEW WAY.

Doris Lessing

Something I understood in a new way today:

_____

_____

_____

_____

_____

_____

Wisdom hears one thing and understands three things.

Chinese proverb

What I heard:

_____

_____

What I understood:

1. _____

2. _____

3. _____

MULTIPLE INTELLIGENCES

Spatial

Linguistic

Logical-Mathematical

Musical Intelligence
is sensitivity to rhythm, pitch, meter, tone, melody, and timbre. It may entail the ability to sing, play musical instruments, and/or compose music.

Bodily-Kinesthetic

Interpersonal

Intrapersonal

Naturalistic

Musical

I learned to identify these birds by their songs:

_____

_____

_____

DATE: __ / __ / __

PLAYING MUSIC IS THE BRAIN'S EQUIVALENT OF A FULL-BODY WORKOUT... PLAYING AN INSTRUMENT ENGAGES PRACTICALLY EVERY AREA OF THE BRAIN AT ONCE.

Glenn Kurtz, attributed

I exercised my brain musically today by

 playing this familiar instrument:

_____

_____

☐ trying this instrument for the first time:

_____

_____

DATE: __ / __ / __

AHA! MOMENT

STEPHEN HAWKING

There is nothing like the eureka moment of discovering something that no one knew before.... One evening ... as I was getting ready for bed ... suddenly I had a revelation about what happens when two black holes collide and merge.

My sudden revelation today:

_____

_____

_____

_____

_____

Eureka!
[I found it!]

Archimedes

Something I found out today:

_____

_____

_____

_____

_____

DATE: __ / __ / __

WHAT I OBSERVED TODAY:

_____

_____

_____

_____

_____

_____

DATE: __ / __ / __

HOW I EXPERIMENTED TODAY:

_____

_____

_____

_____

_____

_____

OBSERVATION
IS A PASSIVE
SCIENCE,
EXPERIMENTATION
IS AN ACTIVE
SCIENCE.

Claude Bernard

To be conscious of one's ignorance is the beginning of wisdom.

N. Sri Ram

What I know I am ignorant about:

_____

_____

_____

_____

_____

ONLY IGNORANCE! ONLY *IGNORANCE*! HOW CAN YOU TALK ABOUT *ONLY* IGNORANCE! DON'T YOU KNOW THAT IT IS THE WORST THING IN THE WORLD, NEXT TO WICKEDNESS.

Anna Sewell

What helped to cure my ignorance today:

_____

_____

_____

_____

_____

The object of the Short-Word Game
is for two or more people to carry on
a conversation using only one-syllable
words. This is not easy to accomplish.

(If you were playing the
game, these instructions would be:
"Talk with a friend or friends and use just
short words. This is quite hard.")

My best short-word sentence today:

_____

_____

_____

_____

_____

_____

An average English word is four letters and a half. By hard, honest labor I've dug all the large words out of my vocabulary and shaved it down till the average is three letters and a half.

Mark Twain

Fill in the rest of Twain's quote and add your own large word to the third prompt:

I never write "metropolis" for seven cents, because I can get the same money for " ____ ____ ____ ____ ."

I never write "policeman," because I can get the same price for " ____ ____ ____ ."

I never write "valetudinarian" at all.

I never write _____ at all.

DID YOU SHOW

MORE PROMISE THAN

E. E. CUMMINGS,

the author of 2,900 poems?

At age 12, he was "excellent" in spelling and
language but only "fair" in writing.

How was your writing judged in childhood?

_____

How do you judge your writing now?

_____

Almost anybody can learn to think or believe or know, but not a single human being can be taught to feel.

e. e. cummings

My untaught feeling today:

_____

_____

_____

_____

_____

Learn, compare, collect the facts!

Ivan Petrovich Pavlov

DATE: __ / __ / __

WHAT I LEARNED TODAY:

_____

_____

_____

DATE: __ / __ / __

WHAT I COMPARED TODAY:

_____

_____

_____

DATE: __ / __ / __

FACTS I COLLECTED TODAY:

_____

_____

_____

Stung by the splendour of a sudden thought.

Robert Browning

A brilliant thought I had today:

_____

_____

_____

_____

_____

Wisdom is not the purchase of a day.

Thomas Paine

A brilliant thought I have been refining for

[_____] days; [_____] months; [_____] years:

_____

_____

_____

_____

STUDY SMART:
The Context Effect

Studies show that people remember more if they study in varied settings—different places, different times of day, different background music. These changes create new associations in the brain and more clues for retrieving the information later.

Settings where I could study:

In memory everything seems to happen to music.

Tennessee Williams

My playlist for studying today:

_____

_____

_____

_____

_____

Make 3 squares by moving 4 matchsticks:

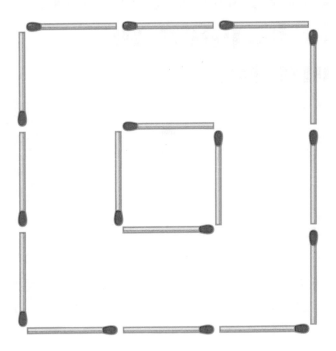

(See *Solutions to Puzzles* at the back of the book.)

Turn these 9 matchsticks into 10
by changing their placement:

IT REQUIRES A VERY UNUSUAL MIND TO UNDERTAKE THE ANALYSIS OF THE OBVIOUS.

Alfred North Whitehead

Analyze this:

Why are there right and left gloves but not right and left socks?

_____

_____

_____

_____

_____

Which line is longer?

Measure:

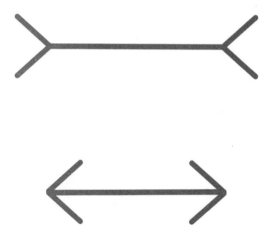

SOUND SMART:
Say It Scientifically

- *catalyst* (something that causes an event)
- *effluvium* (unpleasant odor)
- *fibrillation* (quivering movement)
- *metamorphosis* (transformation from one form into another)
- *transference* (redirection of emotions, often to a psychotherapist)
- *virtualize* (change into a computer-generated simulation of reality)

Use one of these scientific words in a sentence:

It's very hard to talk quantum using a language originally designed to tell other monkeys where the ripe fruit is.

Terry Pratchett

Use language a toddler could understand to explain gravity:

_____

_____

_____

_____

DATE: __/__/__

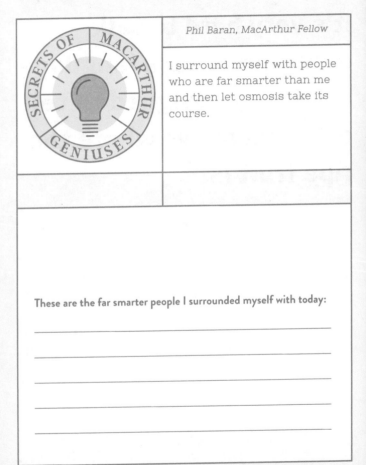

SECRETS OF MACARTHUR GENIUSES

Phil Baran, MacArthur Fellow

I surround myself with people who are far smarter than me and then let osmosis take its course.

These are the far smarter people I surrounded myself with today:

_____

_____

_____

_____

_____

DATE: __ / __ / __

A SINGLE CONVERSATION ACROSS THE TABLE WITH A WISE MAN IS BETTER THAN TEN YEARS' MERE STUDY OF BOOKS.

Henry Wadsworth Longfellow

What I learned in a conversation with _____ today:

_____

_____

_____

_____

_____

DATE: __/__/__

10 PLACES

SMART PEOPLE KNOW

CHECK OFF THE PLACES YOU HAVE VISITED OR READ ABOUT.

- [ ] Bangkok, Thailand
- [ ] Delhi, India
- [ ] Istanbul, Turkey
- [ ] London, United Kingdom
- [ ] New York City, United States
- [ ] Paris, France
- [ ] Rio de Janeiro, Brazil
- [ ] Rome, Italy
- [ ] Singapore
- [ ] Tokyo, Japan

The place I plan to explore next:

The travel impulse is mental and physical curiosity.

Paul Theroux

The place I am most curious about is _____

because: _____

_____

_____

_____

_____

_____

The test of a first-rate intelligence is the ability to hold two opposed ideas in the mind at the same time, and still retain the ability to function.

F. Scott Fitzgerald

DATE: __ / __ / __

AN IDEA I ACCEPT:

_____

_____

_____

_____

_____

_____

DATE: __ / __ / __

AN OPPOSING IDEA I ACCEPT:

_____

_____

_____

_____

_____

_____

Minds are like parachutes. They only function when they are open.

Sir James Dewar, attributed

What I learned when I opened my mind today:

_____

_____

_____

_____

_____

EVERY NOW AND THEN A MAN'S MIND IS STRETCHED BY A NEW IDEA OR SENSATION, AND NEVER SHRINKS BACK TO ITS FORMER DIMENSIONS.

Oliver Wendell Holmes

An idea that expanded my mind forever:

_____

_____

_____

_____

_____

MULTIPLE INTELLIGENCES

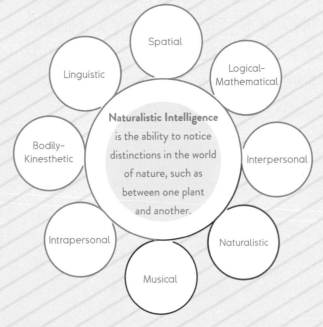

Spatial

Linguistic

Logical-Mathematical

Naturalistic Intelligence is the ability to notice distinctions in the world of nature, such as between one plant and another.

Bodily-Kinesthetic

Interpersonal

Intrapersonal

Naturalistic

Musical

Pick up leaves from two different kinds of trees and compare them:

_____

_____

_____

ACCURACY OF OBSERVATION IS THE EQUIVALENT OF ACCURACY OF THINKING.

Wallace Stevens

Take this book on a walk in the woods or a park today. Fill the page with drawings of what you observe.

FOOD FOR THOUGHT

Spinach and other leafy greens . . . can make your brain function more like the brain of someone who is five years younger.

Cleveland Clinic

I try to eat leafy greens at least _____ times a week.

Today I had:

_____

_____

_____

I'm strong to the finich, 'cause I eats me spinach, I'm Popeye the sailor man! [toot, toot]

Popeye

I was strong to the finich because I ate _____ today.

DATE: __ / __ / __

WHAT I LEARNED TODAY:

_____

_____

_____

DATE: __ / __ / __

WHAT I UNLEARNED TODAY:

_____

_____

_____

DATE: __ / __ / __

WHAT I RELEARNED TODAY:

_____

_____

_____

THE ILLITERATE OF
THE 21ST CENTURY
WILL NOT BE THOSE
WHO CANNOT READ
AND WRITE, BUT
THOSE WHO CANNOT
LEARN, UNLEARN,
AND RELEARN.

Alvin Toffler, attributed

I rarely end up where I was intending to go, but often I end up somewhere that I needed to be.

Douglas Adams

Where I was intending to go today:

_____

_____

_____

Where I ended up:

_____

_____

_____

Go through this maze to end up smarter.

SMART

DATE: __/__/__

THERE IS NOTHING LIKE RETURNING TO A PLACE THAT REMAINS UNCHANGED TO FIND THE WAYS IN WHICH YOU YOURSELF HAVE ALTERED.

Nelson Mandela

How I am different today in a place that has stayed the same:

_____

_____

_____

_____

_____

DATE: __ / __ / __

We shall not cease from exploration

And the end of all our exploring

Will be to arrive where we started

And know the place for the first time.

T. S. Eliot

What I now understand about the place from where I started:

_____

_____

_____

_____

_____

DID YOU SHOW

MORE PROMISE THAN

DR. MARTIN LUTHER KING, JR.,

one of the greatest modern orators?

King received C's in public speaking at his seminary.

How good a public speaker were you in childhood?

_____

How good are you now?

_____

We must remember that intelligence is not enough. Intelligence plus character— that is the goal of true education.

Martin Luther King, Jr.

What I did today that required both intelligence and character:

_____

_____

_____

_____

_____

_____

Tell me and I'll forget. Show me, and I may not remember. Involve me, and I'll understand.

Native American proverb

DATE: __ / __ / __

TODAY I WAS TOLD THIS AND FORGOT:

_____

_____

_____

DATE: __ / __ / __

TODAY I WAS SHOWN THIS AND MAY NOT REMEMBER:

_____

_____

_____

DATE: __ / __ / __

TODAY I WAS INVOLVED IN THIS AND NOW UNDERSTAND:

_____

_____

_____

A hunch is creativity trying to tell you something.

Frank Capra, attributed

Today I had this hunch:

_____

_____

_____

_____

First thought, best thought.

Beat Generation motto

My first thought this morning:

_____

_____

_____

_____

_____

WORK SMART:

Easy-to-Remember Strategies

I. Identify

D. Design

E. Execute

A. Augment

How I used this IDEA to present a new concept:

DATE: __/__/__

YOU'RE ALWAYS WORKING TO IMPROVE, AND YOU'RE ALWAYS BEING CRITIQUED ON YOUR NEXT PERFORMANCE. IT'S NOT ABOUT WHAT YOU'VE DONE. THERE'S ALWAYS ROOM TO GROW.

Misty Copeland

How I improved my performance today:

_____

_____

_____

_____

BRAIN GAME

Convert these 6 visual puns into common phrases.

Example:

3.14159

apple pie

PERSONALITY
PERSONALITY

stood
mis

somewhere

ONCE

chair

IN   VADERS

(See *Solutions to Puzzles* at the back of the book.)

BRAIN GAME

Convert these 6 common words and phrases
into visual puns. Example: History repeats
itself = history, history, history

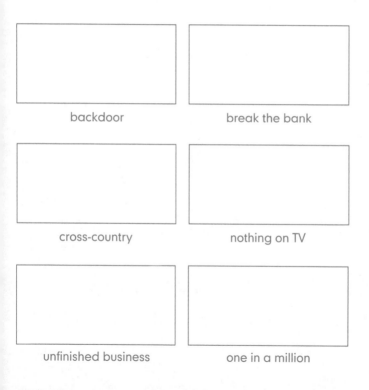

backdoor

break the bank

cross-country

nothing on TV

unfinished business

one in a million

(See *Solutions to Puzzles* at the back of the book.)

YOU KNOW EVERYBODY IS IGNORANT, ONLY ON DIFFERENT SUBJECTS.

Will Rogers

DATE: __ / __ / __

SUBJECTS I AM IGNORANT OF TODAY:

_____

_____

_____

_____

_____

_____

DATE: __ / __ / __

SUBJECTS ON WHICH I WANT TO EDUCATE MYSELF:

_____

_____

_____

_____

_____

_____

The reason why we have two ears and only one mouth is that we may listen the more and talk the less.

Zeno of Citium

What I learned when I was listening today:

_____

_____

_____

_____

_____

It takes a little talent to see clearly what lies under one's nose, a good deal of it to know in which direction to point that organ.

W. H. Auden

Where I pointed my nose today:

_____

_____

_____

_____

_____

DATE: __/__/__

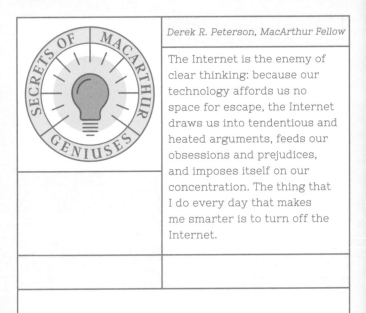

SECRETS OF MACARTHUR GENIUSES

Derek R. Peterson, MacArthur Fellow

The Internet is the enemy of clear thinking: because our technology affords us no space for escape, the Internet draws us into tendentious and heated arguments, feeds our obsessions and prejudices, and imposes itself on our concentration. The thing that I do every day that makes me smarter is to turn off the Internet.

I turned off the Internet for _____ hours today.

How that made me smarter:

_____

_____

_____

COMPUTERS ARE USELESS. THEY CAN ONLY GIVE YOU ANSWERS.

Pablo Picasso

A question with no easy answer that I want to explore in my mind today:

_____

_____

_____

_____

TECH SKILLS

SMART PEOPLE KNOW

10

CHECK OFF THE SKILLS YOU HAVE MASTERED.

- [ ] backup strategies
- [ ] calendar use
- [ ] computer terms (basic)
- [ ] email organization
- [ ] file and photo organization
- [ ] Internet research
- [ ] keyboard shortcuts
- [ ] media literacy
- [ ] privacy and security measures
- [ ] troubleshooting (basic)

The tech skill I plan to learn next:

Computers themselves, and software yet to be developed, will revolutionize the way we learn.

Steve Jobs

Something new I learned with the computer today:

_____

_____

_____

_____

_____

DATE: __ / __ / __

BE PATIENT TOWARD ALL THAT IS UNSOLVED IN YOUR HEART AND TRY TO LOVE THE QUESTIONS THEMSELVES.

Rainer Maria Rilke

An unsolved question in my heart today:

_____

_____

_____

_____

_____

The Two-Door Dilemma

You must choose between two doors. One leads to Heaven and always tells the truth; the other leads to Hell and always lies. You are allowed to ask only one question to one door to discover the way to Heaven. What is your question?

_____

_____

_____

_____

_____

If you only hear one side of the story, you have no understanding at all.

Chinua Achebe

How would a rancher describe meat?

_____

_____

A vegetarian?

_____

_____

A chef?

_____

_____

Travel is fatal to prejudice, bigotry, and narrow-mindedness.

Mark Twain

What I learned from traveling to _____

that opened my mind:

_____

_____

_____

_____

_____

_____

_____

AHA! MOMENT

OPRAH WINFREY

I always love those moments when I sit down to talk to somebody and they say something that makes me look at life or a situation in a completely different way. And I say, "Aha! I get it!" Light bulb! Bing, bing, bing moment. And the little hairs on your arm stand up. *That* is an aha moment.

My bing, bing, bing moment with _____ today:

_____

_____

_____

_____

_____

No him, no me.

▲

**Dizzy Gillespie
(referring to Louis Armstrong)**

▼

No _____, no me.
(person who influenced me most, academically or professionally)

VISION IS THE ART OF SEEING THINGS INVISIBLE.

Jonathan Swift

Something invisible I saw today:

_____

_____

_____

_____

_____

Discovery consists of seeing what everybody has seen and thinking what nobody has thought.

Albert Szent-Györgyi

My discovery today:

_____

_____

_____

_____

_____

What word can be added to the beginning
of all 3 in each set?
Example: trick table board
ANSWER: card

_____ lace horn box

_____ freeze teaser drain

_____ ache pack door

(See *Solutions to Puzzles* at the back of the book.)

What word can be added to the end
of all 3 in each set?
Example: black blue straw
ANSWER: berry

wedding fruit pan   _____

box big carrot   _____

pool picnic multiplication   _____

DATE: __/__/__

Modest doubt is called the beacon of the wise.

William Shakespeare

I modestly doubt that _____.

How I will find the truth:

_____

_____

_____

_____

GREAT INTELLECTS ARE SKEPTICAL.

Friedrich Nietzsche

I am skeptical about _____.

How I will find the truth:

_____

_____

_____

_____

Learn by doing.

Proverb

What I learned by doing today:

_____

_____

_____

_____

_____

DATE: __ / __ / __

Education is an admirable thing,
but it is well to remember from time
to time that nothing that is worth
knowing can be taught.

Oscar Wilde

What I learned today without being taught:

_____

_____

_____

_____

_____

DID YOU SHOW

MORE PROMISE THAN

CHARLOTTE BRONTË,

the author of *Jane Eyre*?

School report: "writes indifferently" and
"knows nothing of grammar."

Did you make up stories in childhood?

_____

_____

Do you make them up now?

_____

_____

Better to be without logic than without feeling.

Charlotte Brontë

How relying on my feelings helped me act smarter today:

_____

_____

_____

_____

_____

_____

My own education operated by a succession of eye-openers each involving the repudiation of some previously held belief.

George Bernard Shaw

DATE: __ / __ / __

MY FIRST EYE-OPENER:

_____

_____

_____

_____

_____

_____

DATE: __ / __ / __

THE NEXT EYE-OPENER:

_____

_____

_____

_____

_____

It is better to ask some of the questions than to know all the answers.

James Thurber

A question I asked today:

_____

_____

_____

_____

_____

Wonder is the beginning of wisdom.

Greek proverb

I wonder:

_____

_____

_____

_____

_____

STUDY SMART:
The Spacing Effect

For more than 100 years researchers have known that in order to master facts, it is better to spread studying over two or three sessions rather than cram it all in the night before an exam. Although the immediate result (the score on the next day's test) may be about the same, learning that is spaced out is retained much longer.

Something I have to learn:

Here is my spaced-out studying plan for learning it:

NO-ONE COULD STUDY MATHEMATICS INTENSIVELY FOR MORE THAN FIVE HOURS A DAY AND REMAIN SANE.

J.B.S. Haldane

Instead of studying _____ intensively for five

hours a day, I will follow this schedule:

_____

_____

_____

_____

_____

BRAIN GAME

Place the numbers 1 to 9 in the circles so that each side of the triangle adds up to 17.

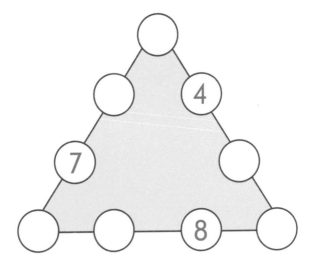

(See *Solutions to Puzzles* at the back of the book.)

BRAIN GAME

Fill this number tower so that every square contains a number. The value of each square is the sum of the 2 squares directly under it.

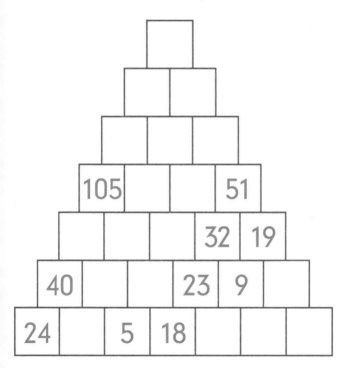

(See *Solutions to Puzzles* at the back of the book.)

DATE: __ / __ / __

MARK THE TIME YOU SPENT TODAY DOING NOTHING.

Start   Finish

DATE: __ / __ / __

IDEA I CAME UP WITH TODAY AFTER DOING NOTHING:

_____

_____

_____

_____

_____

_____

IT TAKES A LOT
OF TIME TO BE
A GENIUS, YOU
HAVE TO SIT
AROUND SO MUCH
DOING NOTHING,
REALLY DOING
NOTHING.

▲
Gertrude Stein
▼

SOUND SMART:
Say It in German

- *Gemütlich* (cozy, comfortable)
- *Schadenfreude* (pleasure derived from another's misfortune)
- *Sturm und Drang* (storm and stress, turmoil)
- *Weltanschauung* (philosophy or view of life)
- *Weltschmerz* (world-weariness, depression)
- *Zeitgeist* (spirit of an age)

Use one of these German words in a sentence:

The limits of my language mean the limits of my world.

Ludwig Wittgenstein

My *Weltanschauung* expanded when I learned this word or phrase today:

_____

_____

_____

_____

DATE: __ / __ / __

	Shannon L. Dawdy, MacArthur Fellow
SECRETS OF MACARTHUR GENIUSES	I go for a walk. Damn the weather. I look up and around. I notice what the plants are doing, how people are feeling, and am ready for a surprise at any turn—a chance encounter, a curious artifact.

What I was surprised by on my walk today:

_____

_____

_____

_____

_____

_____

I HAVE WALKED MYSELF INTO MY BEST THOUGHTS.

Søren Kierkegaard

I walked myself into this great thought today:

_____

_____

_____

_____

_____

_____

_____

DATE: ___/___/___

LITERARY MASTERPIECES
SMART PEOPLE KNOW

10

**CHECK OFF THE BOOKS
YOU HAVE READ.**

☐ *Anna Karenina*, Leo Tolstoy

☐ *Beloved*, Toni Morrison

☐ *Don Quixote*,
Miguel de Cervantes

☐ *In Search of Lost Time*,
Marcel Proust

☐ *Invisible Man*, Ralph Ellison

☐ *Madame Bovary*,
Gustave Flaubert

☐ *One Hundred Years of Solitude*,
Gabriel García Márquez

☐ *Pride and Prejudice*, Jane Austen

☐ *Things Fall Apart*, Chinua Achebe

☐ *Ulysses*, James Joyce

The book I plan to read next:

THAT'S ONE OF THE AMAZING THINGS GREAT BOOKS LIKE THIS [*THE PRICE OF SALT*] DO—THEY DON'T JUST GET YOU TO SEE THE WORLD DIFFERENTLY, THEY GET YOU TO LOOK AT PEOPLE, THE PEOPLE ALL AROUND YOU, DIFFERENTLY.

Will Schwalbe

A book that made me see the people around me differently:

_____

How?

_____

_____

_____

YOU DON'T UNDERSTAND ANYTHING UNTIL YOU LEARN IT MORE THAN ONE WAY.

Marvin Minsky

DATE: __ / __ / __

THE WAY I LEARN BEST:

_____

_____

_____

_____

_____

_____

DATE: __ / __ / __

A SECOND WAY I CAN LEARN:

_____

_____

_____

_____

_____

_____

DATE: __/__/__

I not only use all the brains I have, but all I can borrow.

Woodrow Wilson

People whose brains I borrowed today:

_____

_____

_____

_____

_____

TO ME THE CHARM OF AN ENCYCLOPEDIA IS THAT IT KNOWS—AND I NEEDN'T.

Francis Yeats-Brown, attributed

My go-to "encyclopedia":

_____

_____

_____

_____

MULTIPLE INTELLIGENCES

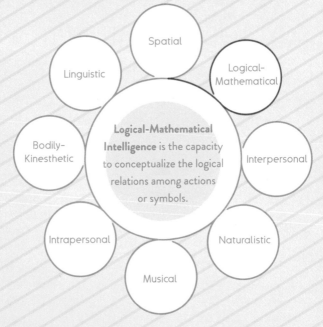

Spatial

Linguistic

Logical-Mathematical

Bodily-Kinesthetic

Logical-Mathematical Intelligence is the capacity to conceptualize the logical relations among actions or symbols.

Interpersonal

Intrapersonal

Naturalistic

Musical

Find the logic in this farmer's pricing:

He sells twelve apples for $6, six apples for $3, and ten apples for $3.

_____

_____

(See *Solutions to Puzzles* at the back of the book.)

FROM A DROP OF WATER A LOGICIAN
COULD INFER THE POSSIBILITY OF AN
ATLANTIC OR A NIAGARA WITHOUT
HAVING SEEN OR HEARD OF ONE OR
THE OTHER.

Sir Arthur Conan Doyle

Walk into the kitchen and logically infer the last thing that happened there:

_____

_____

_____

_____

FOOD
FOR
THOUGHT

Consumption of fish, as well as other types of seafood, seems to benefit cognitive function. This may be due to the omega-3 fatty acid content.

Global
Council on
Brain Health

How many servings of fish I ate this week:

I am a great eater of beef and I believe that does harm to my wit.

William Shakespeare

I have to avoid eating _____

if I need to do deep thinking.

By learning
you will
teach; by
teaching you
will learn.

Latin proverb

DATE: __ / __ / __

WHAT I LEARNED TODAY AND NEED TO TEACH:

_____

_____

_____

_____

_____

_____

DATE: __ / __ / __

WHAT I LEARNED TODAY IN THE COURSE OF TEACHING:

_____

_____

_____

_____

_____

How many bars do you see below?

☐ 3 bars ☐ 4 bars ☐ both

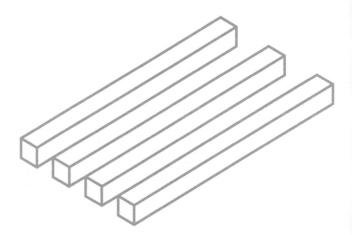

(See *Solutions to Puzzles* at the back of the book.)

It is the mark of an educated mind to be able to entertain a thought without accepting it.

Aristotle, attributed

An idea I considered today without accepting it:

_____

_____

_____

_____

_____

DID YOU SHOW

MORE PROMISE THAN

ELVIS PRESLEY,

the king of rock and roll?

Elvis received a C in music on his
eighth-grade report card.

How well did you do in the arts in school?

_____

And now?

_____

IT JUST HAPPENED. I LIKE TO SING, AND
WELL, I JUST STARTED SINGING AND
FOLKS JUST STARTED LISTENING.
I CAN'T TELL FOLKS THAT I WORKED AND
LEARNED AND STUDIED, AND OVERCAME
DISAPPOINTMENTS, BECAUSE I DIDN'T.

Elvis Presley

I like to _____.

I just started _____

and _____

and _____.

DATE: __ / __ / __

WHAT LEARNING MERELY FILLED MY PAIL TODAY:

_____

_____

_____

_____

_____

_____

DATE: __ / __ / __

WHAT LEARNING LIT MY FIRE TODAY:

_____

_____

_____

_____

_____

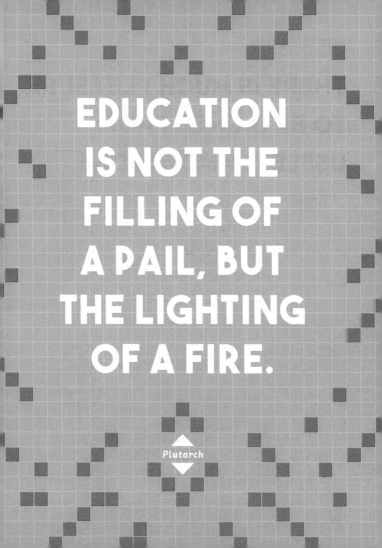

THERE IS MUCH PLEASURE TO BE GAINED FROM USELESS KNOWLEDGE.

Bertrand Russell

A useless piece of knowledge that brought me pleasure today:

_____

_____

_____

_____

_____

The intellect is not a serious thing, and never has been.
It is an instrument on which one plays, that is all.

Oscar Wilde

A silly idea I played with today:

_____

_____

_____

_____

_____

WORK SMART:

Easy-to-Remember Strategies

O. Only
H. Handle
I. It
O. Once

How I used this strategy today:

Until we can manage time we can manage nothing else.

Peter Drucker, attributed

How I managed my time better today:

_____

_____

_____

_____

BRAIN GAME

Spot the odd emoji:

(See *Solutions to Puzzles* at the back of the book.)

BRAIN GAME

What's wrong with this coin?
Find 3 errors:

DATE: __ / __ / __

I FIGURED OUT HOW TO RESOLVE A PERSONAL PROBLEM TODAY:

_____

_____

_____

_____

_____

_____

DATE: __ / __ / __

I FIGURED OUT HOW TO RESOLVE A SOCIAL PROBLEM TODAY:

_____

_____

_____

_____

_____

_____

We only think when we are confronted with a problem.

John Dewey, attributed

WHAT I WANT IS, FACTS. . . . PLANT NOTHING ELSE, AND ROOT OUT EVERYTHING ELSE.

Charles Dickens

A fact that I learned today:

_____

_____

_____

_____

_____

There are not facts, only interpretations.

Friedrich Nietzsche

My new interpretation of what I used to consider a fact:

_____

_____

_____

_____

_____

DATE: __/__/__

SECRETS OF MACARTHUR GENIUSES

Yukiko Yamashita, MacArthur Fellow

Make your own decisions every day and always (by nailing them down to primary information).... By getting used to letting others decide for you, you stop building a logic of your own. If you know you can only rely on yourself, you have to rely on the logic—this realization, the need of being logical, makes you smarter.

A decision I made on my own today:

_____

_____

_____

_____

_____

DARE TO KNOW! HAVE THE COURAGE TO USE YOUR OWN REASON! THIS IS THE MOTTO OF THE ENLIGHTENMENT.

Immanuel Kant

How I used my own reasoning to solve a problem at work today:

_____

_____

_____

_____

_____

DATE: __/__/__

CHECK OFF THE SCIENTIFIC THEORIES YOU KNOW.

SCIENTIFIC THEORIES
SMART PEOPLE KNOW

10

- ☐ atomic theory
- ☐ cell theory
- ☐ climate change
- ☐ evolution
- ☐ game theory
- ☐ information theory
- ☐ oxygen theory of combustion
- ☐ plate tectonics
- ☐ quantum theory
- ☐ theory of relativity

The scientific theory I plan to learn about next:

The good thing about science is that it's true whether or not you believe in it.

Neil deGrasse Tyson

Something scientific that I cannot believe is true:

_____

_____

_____

_____

_____

No man is wise at all times.

Pliny the Elder

DATE: __ / __ / __

WHAT I DID WISELY TODAY:

_____

_____

_____

_____

_____

_____

DATE: __ / __ / __

WHAT I DID UNWISELY TODAY:

_____

_____

_____

_____

_____

_____

I know of no genius but the genius of hard work.

J.M.W. Turner

What I worked on like a genius today:

_____

_____

_____

_____

_____

_____

When I was young, I observed that nine out of ten things I did were failures. So I did ten times more work.

George Bernard Shaw, attributed

What I kept working at today:

_____

_____

How it turned out:

_____

_____

MULTIPLE INTELLIGENCES

Intrapersonal Intelligence is sensitivity to one's own feelings, goals, and anxieties, and the capacity to plan and act in light of one's own traits.

Spatial

Linguistic

Logical-Mathematical

Bodily-Kinesthetic

Interpersonal

Intrapersonal

Naturalistic

Musical

Track one emotion—joy, for example—throughout the day, on a scale of

1 to 10. Emotion: _____

9:00 A.M. _____   12:00 P.M. _____

3:00 P.M. _____   6:00 P.M. _____

DATE: __/__/__

YOU HAVE TO BE ABSOLUTELY FRANK WITH YOURSELF. FACE YOUR HANDICAPS: DON'T TRY TO HIDE THEM. INSTEAD, DEVELOP SOMETHING ELSE.

Audrey Hepburn

My handicap:

_____

_____

What I am developing instead today:

_____

_____

AHA! MOMENT

ALBERT EINSTEIN

I started the conversation . . . in the following way: "Recently I have been working on a difficult problem [in the theory of relativity]. Today I come here to battle against that problem with you." We discussed every aspect of this problem. Then suddenly I understood where the key to this problem lay.

My sounding board today:

_____

My Aha!:

_____

_____

We all need people who will give us feedback. That's how we improve.

Bill Gates

This person improved me today:

_____

_____

_____

_____

_____

DATE: __ / __ / __

HOW A WORK OF ART UPSET MY THINKING TODAY:

_____

_____

_____

_____

_____

_____

DATE: __ / __ / __

HOW LEARNING A SCIENTIFIC FACT REASSURED ME TODAY:

_____

_____

_____

_____

_____

_____

Art
upsets,
science
reassures.

Georges Braque

DATE: __ / __ / __

Think different.

Apple advertising slogan

My different thought today:

_____

_____

_____

_____

_____

Let's put smart to work.

IBM advertising slogan

How I put my smarts to work in solving _____ today:

_____

_____

_____

_____

_____

The true art of memory is the art of attention.

Samuel Johnson

What I will remember from today:

_____

_____

_____

_____

_____

When I meet a man whose name I can't remember, I give myself two minutes; then, if it is a hopeless case, I always say, "And how is the old complaint?"

Benjamin Disraeli, attributed

A trick I use when I cannot remember somene's name:

_____

_____

_____

_____

_____

DID YOU SHOW

MORE PROMISE THAN

HARRY HOUDINI,

the legendary magician?

He went only as far as third grade in his schooling.

How far have you gone in your education? _____

_____

How far do you aim to go: _____

_____

My brain is the key that sets me free.

Harry Houdini

My brain came up with this idea today:

_____

_____

_____

_____

_____

Knowledge comes by taking things apart: analysis. But wisdom comes by putting things together.

John A. Morrison, attributed

DATE: __ / __ / __

WHAT I LEARNED BY TAKING SOMETHING APART TODAY:

_____

_____

_____

_____

_____

_____

DATE: __ / __ / __

WHAT I LEARNED BY PUTTING SOMETHING TOGETHER TODAY:

_____

_____

_____

_____

_____

The Wason Selection Task is a famous logic puzzle.

There are 4 cards in front of you: E, 2, 5, and F. Each card has a number on one side and a letter on the other. Turn over only the cards that can definitively prove or disprove this rule: "If there is an E on one side, the number on the other side must be a 5."

I turned over these cards (circle):

(See *Solutions to Puzzles* at the back of the book.)

THE EXACT OPPOSITE OF WHAT IS GENERALLY BELIEVED IS OFTEN THE TRUTH.

Jean de La Bruyère

Which one of these statements is NOT true?

1. In a room of 23 people, there is a 50 percent chance that 2 of them will have the same birthday.

2. It is safer to skydive than to run a marathon.

3. If a flipped coin lands "heads" 4 times in a row, there is a 25 percent chance that it will land "heads" on the next flip.

4. Coal-burning power plants release more radioactivity into the environment than nuclear power plants.

(See *Solutions to Puzzles* at the back of the book.)

DATE: __/__/__

STUDY SMART:
Digital Danger

Many readers [on digital screens] . . . sample the first line and then word-spot through the rest of the text. When the reading brain skims like this . . . we don't have time to grasp complexity, to understand another's feelings, to perceive beauty, and to create thoughts of the reader's own.   **– Maryanne Wolf, EdD**

My reading today: ☐ _____ percent print

☐ _____ percent digital

☐ _____ percent understood
and retained

The medium is the message.

Marshall McLuhan

What I do differently when I am reading on a screen:

_____

_____

_____

_____

BRAIN GAME

Fill the grid using the 4 numbers below:

3641
3927
6592
6738

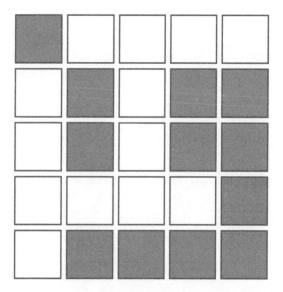

(See *Solutions to Puzzles* at the back of the book.)

Fill the grid using the 4 words below:

IDEA
MUSE
MIND
AHAS

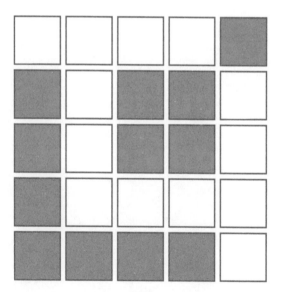

One sure
window into
a person's
soul is his
reading list.

Mary B. W. Tabor

DATE: __ / __ / __

THE BOOKS ON MY BEDSIDE TABLE:

DATE: __ / __ / __

WHAT MY READING LIST SAYS ABOUT ME:

_____

_____

_____

_____

_____

_____

SOUND SMART:
Say It Multisyllabically

- *circumvallate* (surround with a rampart)
- *floccinaucinihilipilification*

  (the estimation of something as worthless)
- *nefarious* (evil)
- *obfuscate* (confuse)
- *perfunctory* (superficial)
- *verisimilitude* (appearance of being real)

Use one of these multisyllabic words in a sentence:

I fear those big words, Stephen said, which make us so unhappy.

James Joyce

Make yourself happy by replacing the big words in Edward Lear's children's verse with little words:

The Strigiformes and the *Felis catus* traversed the hydrospace in a pulchritudinous *Pisum Sativum*-green vessel.

_____

_____

(See *Solutions to Puzzles* at the back of the book.)   **177**

DATE: __ / __ / __

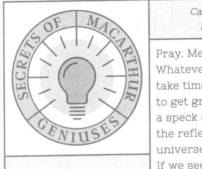

Carlos D. Bustamante,
MacArthur Fellow

Pray. Meditate. Reflect.
Whatever you want to call it;
take time for introspection and
to get grounded. We are both
a speck of cosmic dust and
the reflection of God's (or the
universe's) immense potential.
If we see ourselves as both
small and full of infinite
potential for change, we can
accomplish almost anything
without hubris, pride, and ego.

How I got grounded today:

_____

What I accomplished:

_____

TO SEE A WORLD IN A GRAIN OF SAND
AND A HEAVEN IN A WILD FLOWER
HOLD INFINITY IN THE PALM OF YOUR HAND
AND ETERNITY IN AN HOUR.

William Blake

How being humble helped me accomplish something today:

_____

_____

_____

_____

DATE: __/__/__

CLASSICAL COMPOSERS

10

SMART PEOPLE KNOW

CHECK OFF THE COMPOSERS YOU ALREADY LISTEN TO.

- ☐ *Johann Sebastian Bach*
- ☐ *Ludwig van Beethoven*
- ☐ *Johannes Brahms*
- ☐ *Frédéric Chopin*
- ☐ *Claude Debussy*
- ☐ *George Frideric Handel*
- ☐ *Joseph Haydn*
- ☐ *Wolfgang Amadeus Mozart*
- ☐ *Pyotr Ilyich Tchaikovsky*
- ☐ *Antonio Vivaldi*

The composer I want to listen to next:

*From Mozart I learnt
to say important things
in a conversational way.*

George Bernard Shaw

From _____

I learnt _____.

LEARN FROM
OTHERS WHAT
TO PURSUE AND
WHAT TO AVOID,
AND LET YOUR
TEACHERS BE
THE LIVES
OF OTHERS.

Dionysius Cato

DATE: __ / __ / __

WHAT I LEARNED FROM _____ TO PURSUE:

_____

_____

_____

_____

_____

_____

DATE: __ / __ / __

WHAT I LEARNED FROM _____ TO AVOID:

_____

_____

_____

_____

_____

_____

Never forget . . . that only dead fish swim with the stream.

Malcolm Muggeridge

Today I swam against the stream:

_____

_____

_____

_____

_____

HE DARES TO BE A FOOL, AND THAT IS THE FIRST STEP IN THE DIRECTION OF WISDOM.

James G. Huneker

I dared to be a fool today by:

_____

What I learned:

_____

_____

CURIOSITY . . . IS BUT AN APPETITE AFTER KNOWLEDGE.

John Locke

What I am most curious to learn about today:

_____

_____

_____

_____

_____

I respect faith, but doubt is what gets you an education.

Wilson Mizner

What I discovered because I doubted an accepted truth today:

_____

_____

_____

_____

_____

FOOD FOR THOUGHT

The amino acid called theanine in this brew [tea]—doesn't matter if it's green, black or oolong—is believed to help activate a part of the brain's circuitry that's tied to attention span.

Cleveland Clinic

I drank _____ cups of tea today.

Tea . . . will always be the favorite beverage of the intellectual.

Thomas De Quincey

An intellectual thought I had while drinking tea today:

_____

_____

_____

_____

_____

Only those who do nothing . . . make no mistakes.

Joseph Conrad

What I accomplished today because I dared to make a mistake:

_____

_____

_____

_____

_____

A man of genius makes no mistakes. His errors are volitional and are the portals of discovery.

James Joyce

What I discovered using trial and error today:

_____

_____

_____

_____

_____

Find the 13 triangles in this picture:

(See *Solutions to Puzzles* at the back of the book.)

THE WORLD IS NOT YET EXHAUSTED; LET ME SEE SOMETHING TOMORROW WHICH I NEVER SAW BEFORE.

Samuel Johnson

Something I saw today that I never saw before:

_____

_____

_____

_____

_____

PEOPLE DON'T REALIZE HOW A MAN'S WHOLE LIFE CAN BE CHANGED BY ONE BOOK.

Malcolm X

A book that changed my life:

_____

_____

_____

_____

_____

There is no Frigate like a Book
To take us Lands away.

Emily Dickinson

Where my book took me today:

_____

_____

_____

_____

_____

DID YOU SHOW

MORE PROMISE THAN

JOHN LENNON,

the Beatles singer and songwriter?

"Hopeless. Rather a clown in class. . . .
Certainly on the road to failure."

And they said I was hopeless at:

_____

Ha!

When I was about twelve, I used to think I must be a genius, but nobody's noticed. Either I'm a genius or I'm mad, which is it? "No," I said, "I can't be mad because nobody's put me away; therefore I'm a genius." Genius is a form of madness and we're all that way.

John Lennon

I am a mad genius at:

_____

_____

BRAIN GAME

Decode this Caesar Box to make a sentence.
Hint: Line the letters up to make a box.

Y R A O O E R D U S T A A M T Y.

_ _ _

_ _ _

_ _ _ _ t

_ _ _ _ _ .

(See *Solutions to Puzzles* at the back of the book.)

A GOOD PUZZLE, IT'S A FAIR THING. NOBODY IS LYING. IT'S VERY CLEAR, AND THE PROBLEM DEPENDS JUST ON YOU.

Erno Rubik

Use the numbers from 1 to 9 to fill this magic square.
All the columns, horizontally, vertically, and diagonally,
must add up to 15.

(See *Solutions to Puzzles* at the back of the book.)

WE ARE LIKE DWARVES UPON THE SHOULDERS OF GIANTS, AND SO ABLE TO SEE MORE AND FARTHER THAN THE ANCIENTS.

Bernard of Chartres

The intellectual giants whose shoulders I stand upon:

_____

_____

_____

_____

_____

Our chief want in life is somebody who shall make us do what we can.

Ralph Waldo Emerson

Someone who made me do what I can today:

_____

_____

_____

_____

_____

DATE: __/__/__

WORK SMART:
Easy-to-Remember Strategies

S. Specific
M. Measurable
A. Attainable
R. Realistic
T. Time-bound

Today I set this SMART goal:

When it is obvious that the goals cannot be reached, don't adjust the goals, adjust the action steps.

Confucius

What I need to adjust to reach my goal today: ☐S ☐M ☐A ☐R ☐T

_____

_____

_____

_____

The Sphinx was a mythical monster
that guarded the Greek city of Thebes.
Anyone who tried to enter or leave
had to solve its riddle or die.

Can you solve the riddle of the Sphinx?

What has 4 legs in the morning, 2 at noon, and 3 in the
evening?

_____

_____

_____

(See *Solutions to Puzzles* at the back of the book.)

In Bertrand's Box Paradox,
there are three boxes:

| one contains two gold coins | one contains two silver coins | and one contains a gold coin and a silver coin |

Choose a box at random and withdraw one coin at random. If the coin is a gold coin, what is the probability that the next coin drawn from the same box will also be a gold coin?

_____

_____

_____

DATE: __ / __ / __

KNOWLEDGE THAT GAVE ME PLEASURE TODAY:

_____

_____

_____

_____

_____

_____

DATE: __ / __ / __

KNOWLEDGE THAT GAVE ME POWER TODAY:

_____

_____

_____

_____

_____

_____

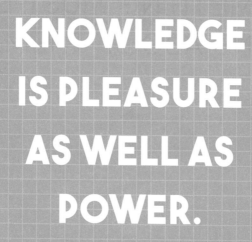

KNOWLEDGE IS PLEASURE AS WELL AS POWER.

William Hazlitt

IDEAS WON'T KEEP. SOMETHING MUST BE DONE ABOUT THEM.

Alfred North Whitehead

What I did with my idea today:

_____

_____

_____

_____

_____

The great end of life is not knowledge but action.

Thomas H. Huxley

My great goal in life is to learn enough to affect:

_____

_____

_____

_____

_____

DATE: __/__/__

DATE: __/__/__

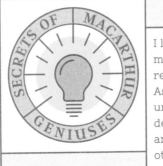

Dawn Song, MacArthur Fellow

I love asking questions; it's my favorite activity, and a really fun, creative process. Asking questions helps me understand things more deeply, connect with others, and see new possibilities that otherwise may be overlooked.

The best question I asked today:

_____

_____

_____

_____

_____

THE ESSENCE OF SCIENCE: ASK AN IMPERTINENT QUESTION, AND YOU ARE ON THE WAY TO THE PERTINENT ANSWER.

Jacob Bronowski

The most impertinent question I asked today:

_____

_____

_____

_____

_____

DATE: ___/___/___

LIFE SKILLS

SMART PEOPLE KNOW

10

CHECK OFF THE LIFE SKILLS YOU HAVE ALREADY MASTERED.

- [ ] car maintenance
- [ ] cooking
- [ ] first aid
- [ ] gardening
- [ ] home repair
- [ ] housecleaning
- [ ] money management
- [ ] outdoor survival
- [ ] swimming and boating
- [ ] tech know-how

The life skill I want to master next:

The purpose of education is to make good human beings with skill and expertise.

A.P.J. Abdul Kalam, *attributed*

A life skill I learned in school:

_____

_____

_____

_____

_____

It is the
province of
knowledge to
speak, and it
is the privilege
of wisdom
to listen.

Oliver Wendell Holmes

DATE: __ / __ / __

WHAT I SPOKE ABOUT KNOWLEDGEABLY TODAY:

_____

_____

_____

_____

_____

_____

DATE: __ / __ / __

WHAT I LEARNED BY LISTENING TODAY:

_____

_____

_____

_____

_____

_____

EVERY NEW IDEA HAS SOMETHING OF THE PAIN AND PERIL OF CHILDBIRTH ABOUT IT.

Samuel Butler

I struggled to give birth to this idea today:

_____

_____

_____

_____

_____

There are few minds in a century that can look upon a new idea without terror.

W. Somerset Maugham

A new idea that terrified me today:

_____

_____

_____

_____

_____

MULTIPLE INTELLIGENCES

Spatial

Linguistic

Logical-
Mathematical

**Spatial
Intelligence** is the
ability to conceptualize and
manipulate large-scale spatial
arrays (e.g., airplane pilot, sailor)
or more local forms of
space (e.g., architect,
chess player).

Bodily-
Kinesthetic

Interpersonal

Intrapersonal

Naturalistic

Musical

Draw a map of the route from your house to work/school.

A ROCK PILE CEASES TO BE A ROCK PILE THE MOMENT A SINGLE MAN CONTEMPLATES IT, BEARING WITHIN HIM THE IMAGE OF A CATHEDRAL.

Antoine de Saint-Exupéry

Crumple a piece of paper. Draw it here as a building:

AHA! MOMENT

GRAHAM GREENE

I believe I've got a book coming [*The Third Man*]. I feel so excited. . . . I walked all up Piccadilly and back and went to a Gent's in Brick Street, and suddenly in the Gent's, I saw the three chunks, the beginning, the middle and the end.

An idea I got in the bathroom today:

_____

_____

_____

_____

_____

I GOT SOME OF MY PLOTS JUST SITTING IN THE BATHTUB, UNDISTURBED, AND LINING THE RIM OF THE TUB WITH APPLE CORES. I'VE GOTTEN OTHERS WALKING, OR WASHING UP THE DISHES.

Agatha Christie

Where I got an idea today:

_____

_____

_____

_____

_____

DATE: __/__/__

HOW MY NEW IDEA WAS KILLED TODAY:

_____

_____

_____

_____

_____

_____

DATE: __/__/__

HOW I WILL REJUVENATE A SLAIN IDEA TODAY:

_____

_____

_____

_____

_____

_____

A NEW IDEA IS DELICATE. IT CAN BE KILLED BY A SNEER OR A YAWN. IT CAN BE STABBED TO DEATH BY A QUIP AND WORRIED TO DEATH BY A FROWN ON THE RIGHT MAN'S BROW.

Charles H. Brower

The best thing for being sad . . . is to learn something.

T. H. White

It made me happy to learn this today:

_____

_____

_____

_____

_____

Thought is the labor of the intellect, reverie is its pleasure.

Victor Hugo

A reverie that gave my mind pleasure today:

_____

_____

_____

_____

_____

We learn only from those whom we love.

Johann Wolfgang von Goethe

What I learned from a loved one today:

_____

_____

_____

_____

_____

It is right to learn even from one's enemies.

Ovid

What I learned from an enemy today:

_____

_____

_____

_____

_____

DID YOU SHOW

MORE PROMISE THAN

LUDWIG VAN BEETHOVEN,

one of the greatest composers of all time?

His music teacher once said of him,
"As a composer, he is hopeless."

Did a teacher ever give up on you?

_____

What would that teacher say now?

_____

MUSIC IS A HIGHER REVELATION THAN ALL WISDOM AND PHILOSOPHY.

Ludwig van Beethoven

What a piece of music revealed to me today:

_____

_____

_____

_____

_____

_____

PEOPLE FIND IDEAS A BORE BECAUSE THEY DO NOT DISTINGUISH BETWEEN LIVE ONES AND STUFFED ONES ON A SHELF.

Ezra Pound

DATE: __ / __ / __

A LIVE IDEA:

_____

_____

_____

_____

_____

_____

DATE: __ / __ / __

A STUFFED IDEA ON A SHELF:

_____

_____

_____

_____

_____

_____

Use the letter in the center of the box twice and every other letter once to make a famous ten-letter name.

(See *Solutions to Puzzles* at the back of the book.)

Make 6 adjectives from this phrase:
EXERCISE YOUR MIND.

_____

_____

_____

_____

_____

_____

STUDY SMART:
The Case for Memorizing

Memorization provides exercise for the mind . . . trains the mind to pay attention and focus intensely . . . trains the brain to develop learning and memory schemas that facilitate future learning. **– William Klemm, PhD**

I memorized this ☐ poem ☐ recipe ☐ phone number
☐ formula ☐ password ☐ _____ today:
                                    (other)

AFTER THE MANNER OF THE
PYTHAGOREANS—TO KEEP MY MEMORY
IN WORKING ORDER—I REPEAT IN THE
EVENING WHATEVER I HAVE SAID, HEARD,
OR DONE IN THE COURSE OF EACH DAY.

Cicero

Here is what I said, heard, or did today that I want to remember:

_____

_____

_____

_____

Mixing one's wines may be a mistake, but old and new wisdom mix admirably.

Bertolt Brecht

DATE: __ / __ / __

AN OLD WISDOM THAT MIXES WITH MY LEARNING TODAY:

_____

_____

_____

_____

_____

_____

DATE: __ / __ / __

A NEW WISDOM THAT MIXES WITH WHAT I ALREADY KNOW:

_____

_____

_____

_____

_____

_____

TO UNDERSTAND IS TO

What number should the question mark be?

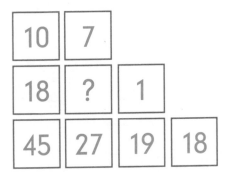

(See *Solutions to Puzzles* at the back of the book.)

PERCEIVE PATTERNS.

◄ *Isaiah Berlin*

Fill in this pattern:

Every time _____

_____

_____

happens in my life, _____

_____

_____

follows.

SOUND SMART:

Say It in Latin

- *bona fide* (authentic)
- *ipso facto* (by the fact itself)
- *mea culpa* (my fault)
- *modus operandi* (way of working)
- *quid pro quo* (trade-off or favor in exchange)
- *sine qua non* (an essential element)

Use one of these Latin phrases in a sentence:

The Romans would never have had time to conquer the world if they had been obliged to learn Latin first of all.

Heinrich Heine

How much time I wasted learning Latin:

_____

_____

_____

_____

DATE: ___/___/___

SECRETS OF MACARTHUR GENIUSES

Shwetak Patel, MacArthur Fellow

In your career, you eventually get to a point that you are so busy that you find yourself saying "no" to almost everything. One thing I have learned is to think about what I will always say "yes" to. This way you get smarter about staying on top of the things that are the most rewarding to you and prioritizing those things.

I will always say "yes" to _____.

THE ART OF BEING WISE IS THE ART OF KNOWING WHAT TO OVERLOOK.

William James

What I wisely overlooked today:

_____

_____

_____

_____

_____

DATE: __/__/__

WESTERN ARTISTS
SMART PEOPLE KNOW

10

CHECK OFF THE ARTISTS WHOSE WORK YOU CAN RECOGNIZE.

- [ ] Leonardo da Vinci
- [ ] Henri Matisse
- [ ] Michelangelo
- [ ] Claude Monet
- [ ] Pablo Picasso
- [ ] Raphael
- [ ] Rembrandt
- [ ] Vincent van Gogh
- [ ] Diego Velázquez
- [ ] Johannes Vermeer

A great artist I want to study next:

I decided to start anew, to strip away what I had been taught.

Georgia O'Keeffe

Draw a self-portrait showing the back of your head.

Without using a pencil, find the word hidden in the grid.
Eliminate all letters that appear more than once.

The word is:

_____

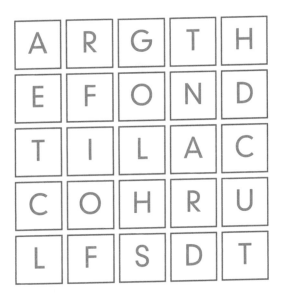

A	R	G	T	H
E	F	O	N	D
T	I	L	A	C
C	O	H	R	U
L	F	S	D	T

(See *Solutions to Puzzles* at the back of the book.)

Make 10 words of 5 or 6 letters each and two
9-letter words to show how smart you are. Each
word must use the letter in the center of the
circle. Letters may be used more than once.

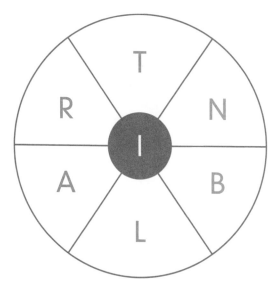

I see mysteries and complications wherever I look.

Martha Gellhorn

A mystery I saw today:

_____

_____

_____

_____

_____

EVERYTHING IS COMPLICATED;
IF THAT WERE NOT SO, LIFE
AND POETRY AND EVERYTHING
ELSE WOULD BE A BORE.

Wallace Stevens

Today's fascinating complication:

_____

_____

_____

_____

_____

MULTIPLE INTELLIGENCES

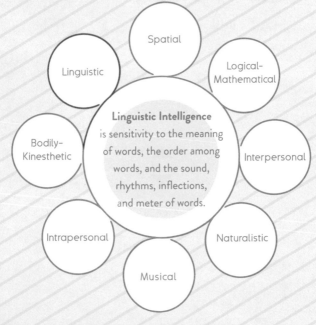

Spatial

Linguistic

Logical-Mathematical

Linguistic Intelligence is sensitivity to the meaning of words, the order among words, and the sound, rhythms, inflections, and meter of words.

Bodily-Kinesthetic

Interpersonal

Intrapersonal

Naturalistic

Musical

Look out your window and write a haiku about something you see.
The verse form is 17 syllables in 3 lines: 5/7/5.

_____

_____

_____

CLARITY IN LANGUAGE DEPENDS ON CLARITY IN THOUGHT.

Arthur M. Schlesinger, Jr.

Explain clearly a difficult concept in a subject area you know well:

_____

_____

_____

_____

_____

FOOD FOR THOUGHT

Research shows that eating blueberries, acai berries, and strawberries may protect against mental decline.

I had _____ servings of berries this week.

Doubtless God could have made a better berry [than the strawberry], but doubtless God never did.

Dr. William Boteler

My favorite brain-healthy berry:

_____

DATE: __ / __ / __

A QUESTION I ASKED TODAY:

_____

_____

_____

_____

_____

_____

DATE: __ / __ / __

AN ANSWER I FOUND OUT FOR MYSELF TODAY:

_____

_____

_____

_____

_____

_____

YOU ARE ALSO ASKING ME QUESTIONS AND I HEAR YOU, I ANSWER THAT I CANNOT ANSWER, YOU MUST FIND OUT FOR YOURSELF.

Walt Whitman

I was brought up to believe that the only thing worth doing was to add to the sum of accurate information in the world.

Margaret Mead

What I added to the sum of accurate information in the world today:

_____

_____

_____

_____

_____

DATE: __ / __ / __

Aristotle could have avoided the mistake of thinking that women have fewer teeth than men by the simple device of asking Mrs. Aristotle to keep her mouth open while he counted.

Bertrand Russell

How I collected information in a simple way today:

_____

_____

_____

_____

_____

[Alice said,] "One can't believe impossible things."

"I daresay you haven't had much practice," said the Queen. "When I was your age, I always did it for half-an-hour a day."

Lewis Carroll

Something impossible that I believe:

_____

_____

_____

_____

_____

THE SECRET OF ALL THOSE WHO MAKE DISCOVERIES IS THAT THEY REGARD NOTHING AS IMPOSSIBLE.

Justus von Liebig

Something I discovered because I knew it wasn't impossible:

_____

_____

_____

_____

_____

DATE: __ / __ / __

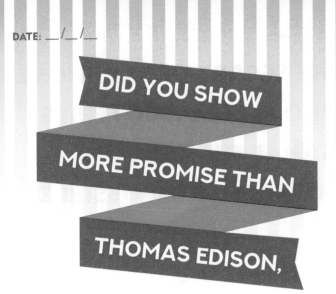

DID YOU SHOW

MORE PROMISE THAN

THOMAS EDISON,

the inventor with 1,093 patents?

His teachers told him he was "too stupid to learn anything."

What did your teachers think about your creativity?

_____

What would they think about your creativity now?

_____

To invent, you need a good imagination and a pile of junk.

Thomas Alva Edison

Invent something from your recycling bin. Draw it here.

A truly great book should be read in youth, again in maturity, and more in old age, as a fine building should be seen by morning light, at noon, and by moonlight.

Robertson Davies

DATE: __ / __ / __

WHAT I THOUGHT OF THIS "TRULY GREAT BOOK" IN MY YOUTH:

_____

_____

_____

_____

_____

DATE: __ / __ / __

WHAT I THINK OF MY YOUTHFUL CHOICE TODAY:

_____

_____

_____

_____

_____

I share no one's ideas. I have my own.

Ivan Turgenev

My own idea today:

_____

_____

_____

_____

_____

I admit that twice two makes four is an excellent thing, but if we are to give everything its due, twice two makes five is sometimes a very charming thing too.

Fyodor Dostoyevsky

A thought I had today that was outside the box:

_____

_____

_____

_____

_____

WORK SMART:

Easy-to-Remember Strategies

F. Follow
O. One
C. Course
U. Until
S. Successful

Today through my FOCUS I succeeded with:

I don't focus on what I'm up against. I focus on my goals and I try to ignore the rest.

Venus Williams

Today I focused on:

_____

_____

_____

_____

_____

BRAIN GAME

Fill each 9-square row, column, and box with the
numbers 1 through 9, using each number only
once in each section.

Easy Sudoku

						2		
3	1		5	4		9		
	4		3					
	7			2		8	3	6
4		3				1		7
8	6	9		1			5	
					7		2	
		8		9	5		7	4
		2						

(See *Solutions to Puzzles* at the back of the book.)

Fill each 9-square row, column, and box with the
numbers 1 through 9, using each number only
once in each section.

Hard Sudoku

				7			3	
7				3	6		9	5
4	9				8		7	
6						9	5	
5								2
	1	8						3
	6		8				4	1
8	7		3	5				9
	4			6				

DATE: __ / __ / __

WHAT I LEARNED IN DOING TODAY:

_____

_____

_____

_____

_____

_____

DATE: __ / __ / __

MY FALL IN THE ROUGH-AND-TUMBLE WORLD TODAY:

_____

_____

_____

_____

_____

_____

Don't learn to do,
but learn in doing.
Let your falls not
be on a prepared
ground, but let
them be *bona fide*
falls in the rough
and tumble of
the world.

Walt Whitman

I INVENT NOTHING.
I REDISCOVER.

Auguste Rodin

An idea I "rediscovered" today:

_____

_____

_____

_____

_____

Utter originality is, of course, out of the question.

Ezra Pound

A not quite utterly original idea I had today:

_____

_____

_____

_____

_____

DATE: __/__/__

SECRETS OF MACARTHUR GENIUSES

Kelly Benoit-Bird, MacArthur Fellow

Try something new every day: take on a new challenge, taste a new food, or do something familiar in a different way. Great insights are often hidden by routine and our brains become more flexible with mental exercise.

Something new I tried today:

_____

_____

_____

_____

_____

_____

DATE: __/__/__

BEHOLD THE TURTLE. HE MAKES PROGRESS ONLY WHEN HE STICKS HIS NECK OUT.

James Bryant Conant, attributed

What I learned when I stuck my neck out today:

_____

_____

_____

_____

_____

_____

WESTERN PHILOSOPHERS

SMART PEOPLE KNOW

10

CHECK OFF THE PHILOSOPHERS YOU KNOW.

- [ ] Aristotle
- [ ] René Descartes
- [ ] Martin Heidegger
- [ ] David Hume
- [ ] Immanuel Kant
- [ ] John Locke
- [ ] Friedrich Nietzsche
- [ ] Plato
- [ ] Socrates
- [ ] Ludwig Wittgenstein

The philosopher I plan to study next:

*I have a simple philosophy.
Fill what's empty.
Empty what's full. And
scratch where it itches.*

Alice Roosevelt Longworth

My simple philosophy:

_____

_____

_____

_____

_____

I MAKE IT
A RULE ONLY
TO BELIEVE
WHAT I
UNDERSTAND.

Benjamin Disraeli

DATE: __ / __ / __

SOMETHING UNUSUAL I BELIEVE BECAUSE I UNDERSTAND IT:

_____

_____

_____

_____

_____

_____

DATE: __ / __ / __

SOMETHING COMMON I DISBELIEVE BECAUSE I DON'T UNDERSTAND IT:

_____

_____

_____

_____

_____

The motto of all the mongoose family is, "Run and find out."

Rudyard Kipling

I ran and found this out today:

_____

_____

_____

_____

_____

DATE: __/__/__

ALL KNOWLEDGE IS OF ITSELF OF
SOME VALUE. THERE IS NOTHING
SO MINUTE OR INCONSIDERABLE
THAT I WOULD NOT RATHER
KNOW IT THAN NOT.

Samuel Johnson

Something minute that I am glad I learned today:

_____

_____

_____

_____

_____

DATE: __/__/__

AHA! MOMENT

PAUL McCARTNEY

I woke up one morning with a tune in my head ["Yesterday"] and I thought, "Hey, I don't know this tune—or do I?"

I woke up this morning with _____ in my head.

The Muses love the Morning, and that is a fit Time for Study.

Erasmus

I got up early to study _____.

The Muses ☐ were ☐ were not with me.

INTELLIGENCE IS QUICKNESS TO APPREHEND AS DISTINCT FROM ABILITY, WHICH IS CAPACITY TO ACT WISELY ON THE THING APPREHENDED.

Alfred North Whitehead

DATE: __ / __ / __

HOW I SHOWED MY INTELLIGENCE TODAY:

_____

_____

_____

_____

_____

_____

DATE: __ / __ / __

HOW I SHOWED MY ABILITY TODAY:

_____

_____

_____

_____

_____

_____

MENTALLY, FALLOW IS AS IMPORTANT AS SEEDTIME. EVEN BODIES CAN BE EXHAUSTED BY OVERCULTIVATION.

George Bernard Shaw

What I did to rest my mind today:

_____

_____

_____

_____

_____

When all is said and done, monotony may after all be the best condition for creation.

Margaret Sackville

What I created on this monotonous day:

_____

_____

_____

_____

_____

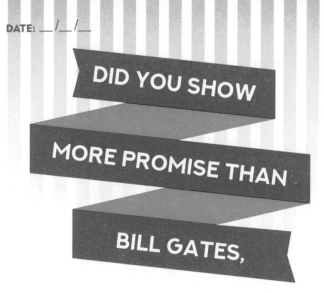

DID YOU SHOW

MORE PROMISE THAN

BILL GATES,

one of the most successful tech entrepreneurs in the world?

He reflected: "I failed in some subjects in exam, but my friend passed in all. Now he is an engineer in Microsoft and I am the owner of Microsoft."

Did you fail any subjects in school? _____

Compare yourself now to your most-likely-to-succeed classmate:

_____

Success is a lousy teacher. It seduces smart people into thinking they can't lose.

Bill Gates

What I learned from a failure today:

_____

_____

_____

_____

_____

DATE: __ / __ / __

SOMETHING DIFFICULT FOR OTHERS THAT I CAN DO EASILY:

_____

_____

_____

_____

_____

_____

DATE: __ / __ / __

SOMETHING IMPOSSIBLE FOR ANYONE ELSE THAT

I ☐ CAN DO   ☐ AM STRIVING FOR:

_____

_____

_____

_____

_____

To do easily
what is difficult
for others is the
mark of talent.
To do what is
impossible for
talent is the
mark of genius.

Henri-Frédéric Amiel

The aim of all education is, or should be, to teach people to educate themselves.

Arnold J. Toynbee

How I educated myself today:

_____

_____

_____

_____

_____

MY EDUCATION WAS THE LIBERTY
I HAD TO READ INDISCRIMINATELY
AND ALL THE TIME, WITH MY EYES
HANGING OUT.

Dylan Thomas

My education was:

_____

_____

_____

_____

_____

STUDY SMART:

Sleep Learning

Benedict Carey (*How We Learn*) reports research that "sleep improves retention and comprehension of what was studied the day before," and that subject matter can be matched to the stage of sleep. Studying for a foreign language test? Go to bed early and review in the morning. A math test? Review before going to bed and then sleep in.

Last night I studied _____

and went to bed at _____.

The result:

Sometimes dreams are wiser than waking.

Black Elk

What I learned while I dreamt last night:

_____

_____

_____

_____

_____

THERE IS MORE BEAUTY IN THE
WORKS OF A GREAT GENIUS, WHO
IS IGNORANT OF ALL THE RULES OF
ART, THAN IN THE WORKS OF A LITTLE
GENIUS, WHO NOT ONLY KNOWS BUT
SCRUPULOUSLY OBSERVES THEM.

Joseph Addison

What I discovered today because I was ignorant of the rules:

_____

_____

_____

_____

_____

DATE: __ / __ / __

[ON LABORATORY RULES]:

HELL! THERE *AIN'T* NO RULES AROUND HERE! WE'RE TRYIN' TO ACCOMPLISH SOMEP'N!

Thomas Alva Edison

Somep'n I accomplished today because there were no rules:

_____

_____

_____

_____

_____

There are two kinds of talent, man-made talent and God-given talent. With man-made talent you have to work very hard. With God-given talent, you just touch it up once in a while.

Pearl Bailey

DATE: __ / __ / __

A MAN-MADE TALENT I HAVE:

_____

_____

_____

_____

_____

_____

DATE: __ / __ / __

A GOD-GIVEN TALENT I HAVE:

_____

_____

_____

_____

_____

_____

The object of opening the mind, as of opening the mouth, is to shut it again on something solid.

G. K. Chesterton

Something solid I shut my mind on today:

_____

_____

_____

_____

_____

If you keep your mind sufficiently open, people will throw a lot of rubbish into it.

William Orton

Other people's mental rubbish I discarded today:

_____

_____

_____

_____

_____

SOUND SMART:
Quote Shakespeare

- *This above all—to thine own self be true.* (Hamlet)

- *Some are born great, some achieve greatness, and some have greatness thrust upon 'em.* (Twelfth Night)

- *Lord, what fools these mortals be!*

  (A Midsummer Night's Dream)

- *Cowards die many times before their deaths:*
  The valiant never taste of death but once.

  (Julius Caesar)

- *All the world's a stage,*
  And all the men and women merely players.

  (As You Like It)

How I used the quote from _____

by Shakespeare today:

I always have a quotation for everything—it saves original thinking.

Dorothy L. Sayers

To win an argument, I used my favorite quotation today:

_____

_____

_____

_____

DATE: __ / __ / __

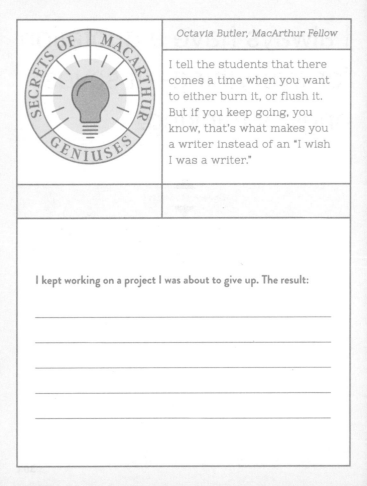

SECRETS OF MACARTHUR GENIUSES

Octavia Butler, MacArthur Fellow

I tell the students that there comes a time when you want to either burn it, or flush it. But if you keep going, you know, that's what makes you a writer instead of an "I wish I was a writer."

I kept working on a project I was about to give up. The result:

_____

_____

_____

_____

_____

THE WORKS OF GENIUS ARE WATERED WITH TEARS.

Honoré de Balzac

I worked to tears today on:

_____

_____

_____

_____

_____

_____

DATE: __/__/__

DATES IN MODERN WESTERN HISTORY

SMART PEOPLE KNOW

10

Add the date of a historical event since 2001: _____

_____

Those who cannot remember the past are condemned to repeat it.

George Santayana

We should/should not do _____ now,

because of what happened in _____.

Nothing is too small to know, and nothing too big to attempt.

William Van Horne

DATE: __ / __ / __

SOMETHING VERY SMALL THAT I KNOW:

_____

_____

_____

_____

_____

_____

DATE: __ / __ / __

SOMETHING VERY BIG THAT I WILL ATTEMPT TODAY:

_____

_____

_____

_____

_____

_____

ALL OUR TALENTS INCREASE IN THE USING, AND EVERY FACULTY, BOTH GOOD AND BAD, STRENGTHENS BY EXERCISE.

Anne Brontë

How I exercised a good faculty today:

_____

_____

_____

_____

_____

Life is like a ten-speed bicycle. Most of us have gears we never use!

Charles Schulz, attributed

A new mental gear I tried out today:

_____

_____

_____

_____

_____

MULTIPLE INTELLIGENCES

Spatial

Linguistic

Logical-Mathematical

Bodily-Kinesthetic Intelligence is the ability to use one's whole body, or parts of the body (like the hands or the mouth), to solve problems or create products.

Bodily-Kinesthetic

Interpersonal

Intrapersonal

Naturalistic

Musical

Today I used my ☐ hands ☐ legs ☐ feet ☐ whole body to _____

_____

_____

_____.

THE MOVEMENT
NEVER LIES.

George Graham

When you wake up, stretch as high above your head as you can. Then stretch as far down toward your feet as you can. What did you learn from these movements?

_____

_____

_____

_____

_____

FOOD FOR THOUGHT

Studies show that nuts and seeds are excellent sources of vitamin E, which can help prevent mental decline as you age.

My go-to nuts and seeds:

_____

_____

_____

_____

Don't eat anything your great-grandmother wouldn't recognize as food.

Michael Pollan

Circle the products your great-grandmother would recognize as foods:

DATE: __ / __ / __

A SUBJECT I KNOW MYSELF:

_____

_____

_____

_____

_____

_____

DATE: __ / __ / __

WHERE I FOUND INFORMATION ABOUT _____ TODAY:

_____

_____

_____

_____

_____

_____

Knowledge is
of two kinds.
We know a
subject ourselves,
or we know
where we can
find information
upon it.

Samuel Johnson

[HOW DID YOU DISCOVER THE LAW OF GRAVITATION?]

BY THINKING ABOUT IT ALL THE TIME.

Sir Isaac Newton

A problem I am thinking about all the time:

_____

_____

_____

_____

_____

If people knew how hard
I have had to work to gain
my mastery, it wouldn't
seem so wonderful.

Michelangelo, attributed

How hard I worked to master _____ :

_____

_____

_____

_____

_____

There are worse crimes than burning books. One of them is not reading them.

Joseph Brodsky

I finally opened the cover of this must-read book today:

_____

_____

_____

_____

_____

BOOKS ARE GOOD ENOUGH
IN THEIR OWN WAY, BUT THEY
ARE A MIGHTY BLOODLESS
SUBSTITUTE FOR LIFE.

Robert Louis Stevenson

What life taught me today:

_____

_____

_____

_____

_____

DID YOU SHOW

MORE PROMISE THAN

CHARLES DARWIN,

one of the most influential scientific minds of all time?

He wrote about himself, "I was considered by all my masters and by my father as a very ordinary boy, rather below the common standard in intellect."

What did your teachers and parents think of you as a student growing up?

_____

What would they think of you as a learner now?

_____

A man who dares to waste one hour of time has not discovered the value of life.

Charles Darwin

What I did with my 24 hours today:

_____

_____

_____

_____

_____

AN IDEA IS SALVATION BY IMAGINATION.

Frank Lloyd Wright

DATE: __ / __ / __

MY IDEA FOR MAKING THE WORLD MORE JUST:

_____

_____

_____

_____

_____

_____

DATE: __ / __ / __

MY IDEA FOR MAKING THE WORLD MORE BEAUTIFUL:

_____

_____

_____

_____

_____

WHY DON'T YOU LEARN FROM MY MISTAKES? IT TAKES HALF YOUR LIFE TO LEARN FROM YOUR OWN.

Shelagh Delaney

I learned this from _____'s mistake today:

_____

_____

_____

_____

_____

If I had to live my life again, I'd make the same mistakes, only sooner.

Tallulah Bankhead

I wish I had made this mistake sooner:

_____

_____

_____

_____

_____

DATE: __/__/__

WORK SMART:
Easy-to-Remember Strategies

T. Together
E. Everyone
A. Achieves
M. More

What we achieved today, as a TEAM:

Find a group of people who challenge and inspire you, spend a lot of time with them, and it will change your life.

Amy Poehler

My team:

_____

_____

_____

_____

BRAIN GAME

Find the hidden proverb by changing
one letter in each word:

TOOLS RUST ON THERE ANGERS TEAR NO BREAD.

=

_____

_____

_____

(See *Solutions to Puzzles* at the back of the book.)

With a crossword, we're challenging ourselves to create order out of chaos.

Will Shortz

Pick a type of puzzle you usually do. Bump it up one level. Result:

_____

_____

_____

_____

_____

A MAN SHOULD KEEP HIS LITTLE BRAIN-ATTIC STOCKED WITH ALL THE FURNITURE THAT HE IS LIKELY TO USE, AND THE REST HE CAN PUT AWAY IN THE LUMBER-ROOM OF HIS LIBRARY, WHERE HE CAN GET IT IF HE WANTS IT.

Sir Arthur Conan Doyle

DATE: __ / __ / __

SOMETHING I STORED IN MY BRAIN-ATTIC TODAY:

_____

_____

_____

_____

_____

_____

DATE: __ / __ / __

SOMETHING I PUT AWAY IN THE LUMBER-ROOM OF MY LIBRARY TODAY:

_____

_____

_____

_____

_____

_____

The imagination needs moodling—long, inefficient, happy idling, dawdling and puttering.

Brenda Ueland

What I thought up after a day of moodling:

_____

_____

_____

_____

_____

One must still have chaos in oneself, to give birth to a dancing star.

Friedrich Nietzsche

What my inner chaos gave birth to today:

_____

_____

_____

_____

_____

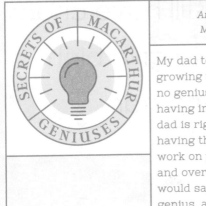

Angela Duckworth,
MacArthur Fellow

My dad told me when I was growing up, "You know, you're no genius." . . . If genius is having inborn talent, then my dad is right. But if genius is having the focus and grit to work on your own weaknesses and overcome them, then I would say, "Dad, you are a genius, and so am I, and so can everyone be if they choose to be."

Weaknesses I have worked on and overcome:

_____

_____

_____

_____

ONE IS NOT BORN A GENIUS: ONE BECOMES A GENIUS.

Simone de Beauvoir

What I did today to become a genius:

_____

_____

_____

_____

ARCHITECTURAL MASTERPIECES

10 SMART PEOPLE KNOW

CHECK OFF THE GREAT BUILDINGS YOU HAVE SEEN IN PERSON OR IN A PHOTO

- ☐ Colosseum, Rome
- ☐ Empire State Building, New York
- ☐ Great Pyramid, Giza
- ☐ Guggenheim Museum, Bilbao
- ☐ Hagia Sophia, Istanbul
- ☐ Notre-Dame, Paris
- ☐ Opera House, Sydney
- ☐ Parthenon, Athens
- ☐ Sagrada Família, Barcelona
- ☐ Taj Mahal, Agra

The building I plan to study next:

We shape our buildings, and afterwards our buildings shape us.

Winston Churchill

How being inside _____ today affected me:

_____

_____

_____

_____

_____

_____

Knowledge is happiness, because to have knowledge—broad, deep knowledge—is to know true ends from false, and lofty things from low.

Helen Keller

DATE: __ / __ / __

A TRUE END I KNOW:

_____

_____

_____

_____

_____

_____

DATE: __ / __ / __

A LOFTY THING I KNOW:

_____

_____

_____

_____

_____

_____

Ideas that enter the mind under fire remain there securely and forever.

Leon Trotsky

An idea that entered my mind under fire today:

_____

_____

_____

_____

_____

To be in the weakest camp is to be in the strongest school.

G. K. Chesterton

What I learned fighting for an unpopular idea today:

_____

_____

_____

_____

_____

MULTIPLE INTELLIGENCES

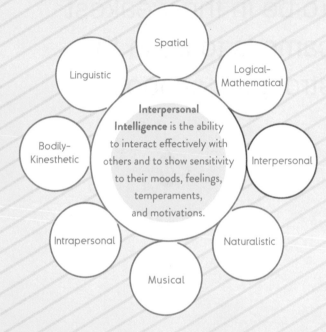

Spatial

Linguistic

Logical-Mathematical

Interpersonal Intelligence is the ability to interact effectively with others and to show sensitivity to their moods, feelings, temperaments, and motivations.

Bodily-Kinesthetic

Interpersonal

Intrapersonal

Naturalistic

Musical

How I used my people smarts to be effective today:

_____

_____

_____

YOU NEVER REALLY UNDERSTAND A PERSON UNTIL YOU . . . CLIMB INTO HIS SKIN AND WALK AROUND IN IT.

Harper Lee

How I finally got to understand _____ today:

_____

_____

_____

_____

_____

If a man does not keep pace with his companions, perhaps it is because he hears a different drummer. Let him step to the music which he hears, however measured or far away.

Henry David Thoreau

The different drummer I heard today:

_____

_____

_____

_____

_____

Be daring, be different, be impractical, be anything that will assert integrity of purpose and imaginative vision against the play-it-safers, the creatures of the commonplace, the slaves of the ordinary.

Cecil Beaton

How I was daring today:

_____

_____

_____

_____

_____

TOPIC:

DATE: __/__/__

WHAT I KNOW:

DATE: __/__/__

WHAT I DON'T KNOW:

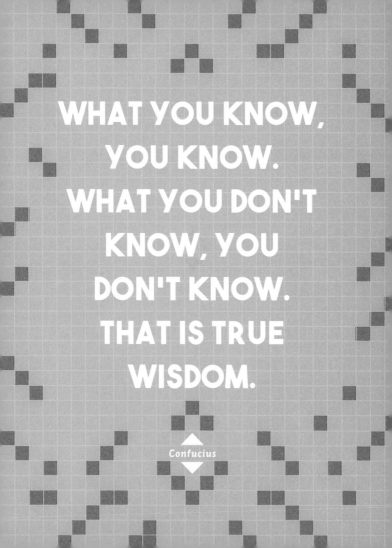

WHAT YOU KNOW,
YOU KNOW.
WHAT YOU DON'T
KNOW, YOU
DON'T KNOW.
THAT IS TRUE
WISDOM.

Confucius

NEVER STAY UP ON THE BARREN HEIGHTS OF CLEVERNESS, BUT COME DOWN INTO THE GREEN VALLEYS OF SILLINESS.

Ludwig Wittgenstein

What I discovered while being silly today:

_____

_____

_____

_____

_____

Nonsense wakes up the brain cells.

Dr. Seuss

What nonsense made me smarter today:

_____

_____

_____

_____

_____

THE DIFFICULTY LIES, NOT IN THE NEW IDEAS, BUT IN ESCAPING FROM THE OLD ONES.

John Maynard Keynes

An old idea I escaped today:

_____

_____

_____

_____

_____

Keep Mozart. . . . Keep Moses too, and Buddha and Lao tse and Christ. Keep them in your heart. But make room for the others, the coming ones, the ones who are already scratching on the window-panes.

Henry Miller

A new intellectual giant who is scratching on my windowpane today:

_____

_____

_____

_____

_____

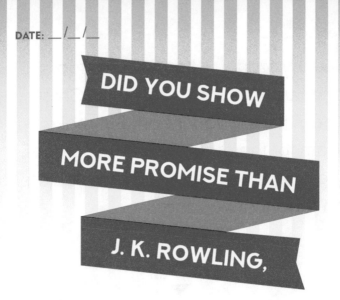

DID YOU SHOW

MORE PROMISE THAN

J. K. ROWLING,

the author of the bestselling Harry Potter books?

Rowling graduated from college with a steady C average.

Were you just an average student in college?

_____

What is your special talent now?

_____

It is our choices, Harry, that show what we truly are, far more than our abilities.

J. K. Rowling

This choice made me stand out:

_____

_____

_____

_____

_____

_____

BRAIN GAME

Draw this figure in one continuous
line without lifting your pencil and without
going over the same lines.

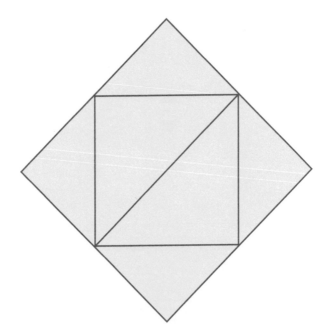

(See *Solutions to Puzzles* at the back of the book.)

Genius, in truth, means little more than the faculty of perceiving in an unhabitual way.

William James

What do you see—a vase or 2 faces?

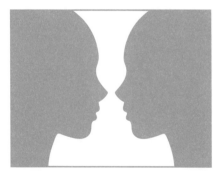

The man who never alters his opinion is like standing water, and breeds reptiles of the mind.

William Blake

A stagnant opinion I changed today:

_____

_____

_____

_____

_____

The only means of strengthening one's intellect is to make up one's mind about nothing—to let the mind be a thoroughfare for all thoughts.

John Keats

Conflicting thoughts I considered on a single topic today:

_____

_____

_____

_____

_____

DATE: __ / __ / __

SECRETS OF MACARTHUR GENIUSES

Julia Wolfe, MacArthur Fellow

It makes me smarter to do a small kindness. We can get so caught up in our own whirl-winds. When I take a moment to check up on a friend, reach out to someone who is struggling either physically or emotionally, really listen and give someone a moment, then I remind myself what it means to be human. Acts of kindness are healing to both giver and receiver. We enrich our hearts and minds—and become much much smarter.

A small kindness I did today:

_____

_____

_____

THE HIGHEST FORM OF WISDOM IS KINDNESS.

Talmud

What I discovered when I did an act of kindness today:

_____

_____

_____

_____

It is not enough for me to ask questions; I want to know how to answer the one question that seems to encompass everything I face: What am I here for?

Abraham Joshua Heschel

DATE: __ / __ / __

WHAT AM I HERE FOR?

_____

_____

_____

_____

_____

_____

DATE: __ / __ / __

ANOTHER ALL-ENCOMPASSING QUESTION I HAVE:

_____

_____

_____

_____

_____

_____

DATE: __ / __ / __

How smart do you feel today, after *doing one thing every day that makes you smarter?*

_____

This is the most ☐ useful ☐ surprising ☐ reassuring thing I learned:

_____

_____

_____

Give yourself a grade: ☐ A
☐ B
☐ C
☐ D
☐ F
☐ Incomplete

SOLUTIONS
TO
PUZZLES

p. 14

One man has a handlebar moustache and full head of hair, and the other is bald with a beard.

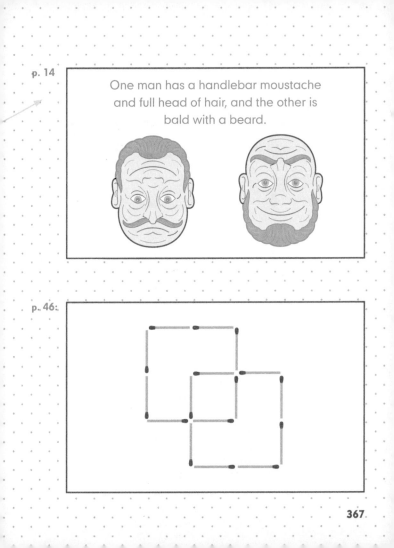

p. 46:

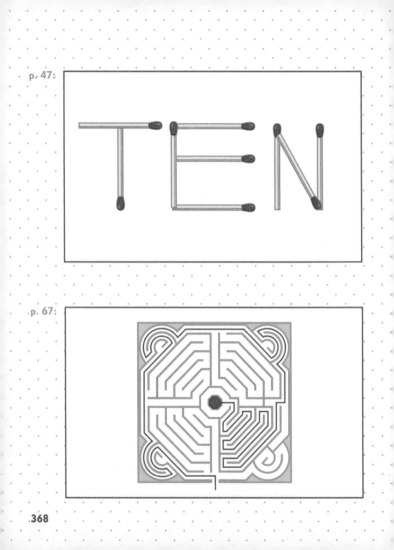

p. 47:

p. 67:

p. 78

split personality,
misunderstood,
somewhere over the rainbow,
once upon a time,
high chair,
space invaders

p. 79

ЯOOꓷ	BA NK
COUNTRY COUNTRY	O TV
BUSINES	MIL1LION

p. 89

"If you were the liar, would you tell me this door leads to Heaven?"

p. 96

shoe, brain, back

p. 97

cake, top, table

p. 110

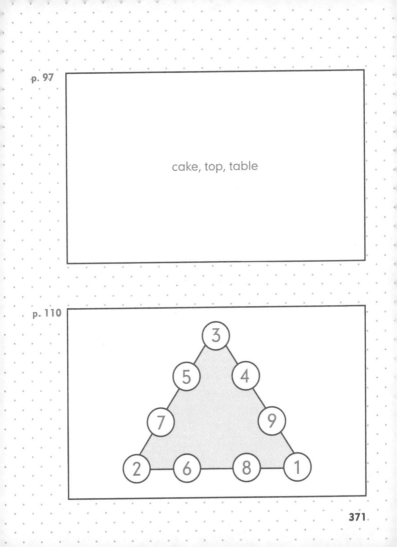

p. 111

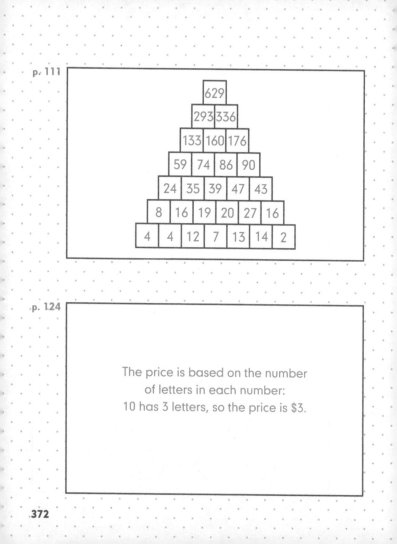

```
                629
             293   336
          133  160  176
        59   74   86   90
      24  35   39  47   43
    8   16  19   20   27  16
  4   4   12   7   13   14   2
```

p. 124

The price is based on the number
of letters in each number:
10 has 3 letters, so the price is $3.

p. 130

Both: Starting from the upper left, you see 4 bars; starting from the lower right, you see 3 bars.

p. 140

The emoji with square glasses is the odd one out!

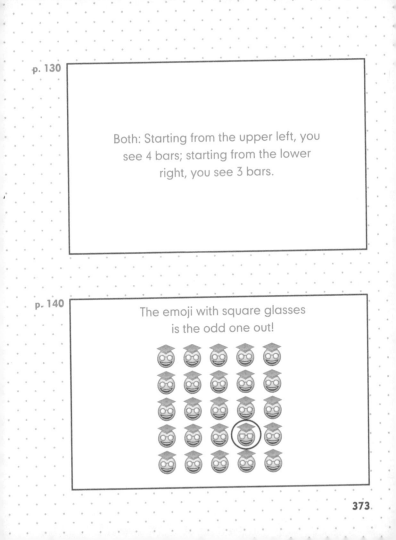

p. 141

One column is missing;
UNUM is misspelled;
should be UNITED (not UNTIED).

p. 168

Turn over E and 2.

p. 169

#3 (flipped coin)

p. 172

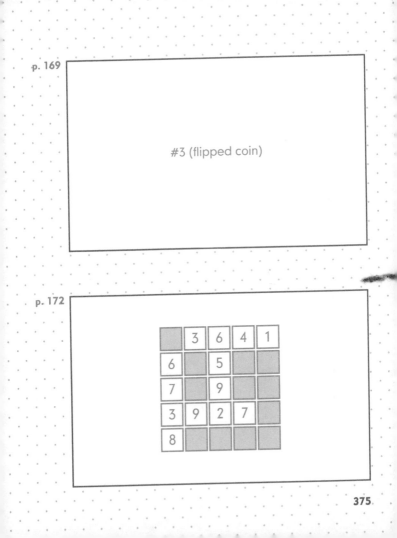

	3	6	4	1
6		5		
7		9		
3	9	2	7	
8				

p. 173

	M	I	N	D	
		D			M
		E			U
		A	H	A	S
					E

p. 177

"The Owl and the Pussy-cat went to sea in a beautiful pea-green boat."

p. 192

10 triangles easy to count (6 red and 3 white, plus the whole figure), plus the top 3 red and 1 white, the lower left 3 red and 1 white, and the lower right 3 red and 1 white.

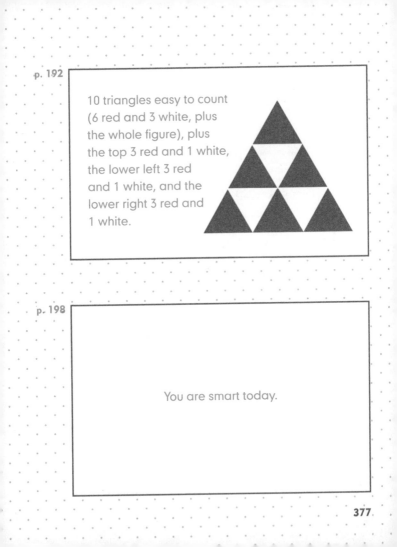

p. 198

You are smart today.

p. 199

4	9	2
3	5	7
8	1	6

p. 204

A human being crawls on all fours as a baby, stands on 2 legs as an adult, and uses a cane in old age.

p. 205

The probability is 2 out of 3. The first coin was gold, so you know you picked either box one or box three. You don't know which one it is, but it is twice as likely to be box one, because that box has twice as many gold coins.

p. 232

WASHINGTON

p. 233

demure, ironic, sexy, sincere,
modern, nerdy

p. 238

? = 8
To get a target number, add together
the number above and the number
to the right of the target number.

p. 246

GENIUS

p. 247

5- and 6-letter words:
RABBIT, ATRIAL, LARIAT, TRIBAL,
ALIBI, BRAIN, BRIAR, LIBRA,
RABBI, TAINT, TRIAL, TRAIN,
TRAIT, TRAIL, TRILL

9-letter words:
BRILLIANT and LIBRARIAN

p. 268

9	8	5	1	7	6	2	4	3
3	1	7	5	4	2	9	6	8
2	4	6	3	8	9	7	1	5
5	7	1	9	2	4	8	3	6
4	2	3	6	5	8	1	9	7
8	6	9	7	1	3	4	5	2
6	9	4	8	3	7	5	2	1
1	3	8	2	9	5	6	7	4
7	5	2	4	6	1	3	8	9

p. 269

1	5	6	9	7	2	8	3	4
7	8	2	4	3	6	1	9	5
4	9	3	5	1	8	2	7	6
6	2	7	1	4	3	9	5	8
5	3	4	6	8	9	7	1	2
9	1	8	7	2	5	4	6	3
2	6	5	8	9	7	3	4	1
8	7	1	3	5	4	6	2	9
3	4	9	2	6	1	5	8	7

p. 330

Fools rush in where angels fear
to tread.

p. 356

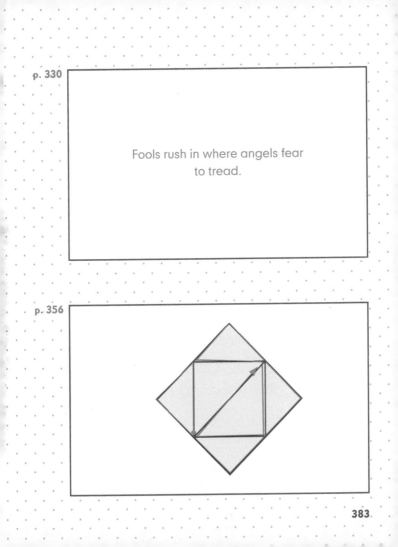

Copyright © 2021 by ROBIE LLC

All rights reserved.
Published in the United States by Clarkson Potter/Publishers,
an imprint of Random House, a division of
Penguin Random House LLC, New York.
clarksonpotter.com

CLARKSON POTTER is a trademark and POTTER with colophon
is a registered trademark of Penguin Random House LLC.

Grateful acknowledgment is made to Howard Gardner for
permission to use the multiple intelligence definitions from MI
Oasis (multipleintelligencesoasis.org) and to the MacArthur Fellows
for the ideas they contributed to this book.

The Sudoku puzzles in this book were created at OpenSky Sudoku
Generator (opensky.ca) and published with permission.

ISBN 978-1-9848-2327-4

Printed in China

Conceived and compiled by Dian G. Smith and Robie Rogge
Book design by Nicole Block
Illustrations by Eyewash

10 9 8 7 6 5 4 3 2 1

First Edition